# More Praise for *101 Exercises for the Soul*

"I have always admired Dr. Bernie Siegel as one of the most remarkable minds of our time. He combines an analytical scientific mind with a deep knowingness of spirituality. His *101 Exercises for the Soul* will help you understand and learn from that part of you which is the ultimate and supreme genius and mirrors the wisdom of the universe."

— Deepak Chopra, author of *The Book of Secrets*

"A beautiful, heartfelt book by a legendary physician to help you nurture mind, body, and soul."

— Judith Orloff, MD,
author of *Second Sight* and *Positive Energy*

"I've often said to myself, 'If only God had written a how-to book explaining how to live on earth. We should all have been given the instruction manual the minute we were born.' Well, God did write the ultimate how-to book, but he wrote it through Dr. Bernie Siegel. In *101 Exercises for the Soul*, America's most beloved doctor shares the wit and wisdom that every human being craves. This delightful book should be required reading for all people everywhere! Read it and learn to live with more joy, balance, purpose, and power directed in ways that bless others. Well done, Bernie! Thanks for spilling the magic beans!"

— Amelia Kinkade,
author of *Straight from the Horse's Mouth*

# *101*
## Exercises
### for the
# Soul

## Other Books by Dr. Bernie S. Siegel

*Love, Medicine & Miracles*

*Help Me to Heal*

*How to Live between Office Visits*

*Peace, Love & Healing*

*Prescriptions for Living*

*Smudge Bunny*

*365 Prescriptions for the Soul*

# *101* Exercises for the Soul

## A Divine Workout Plan
## for Body, Mind, and Spirit

# Dr. Bernie S. Siegel

NEW WORLD LIBRARY
NOVATO, CALIFORNIA

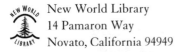 New World Library
14 Pamaron Way
Novato, California 94949

Text design and typography by Tona Pearce Myers

Library of Congress Cataloging-in-Publication Data
Siegel, Bernie S.
  101 exercises for the soul : a divine workout plan for body, mind, and spirit / by Bernie Siegel.— 1st ed.
      p.   cm.
  ISBN-13: 978-1-57731-511-7 (hardcover : alk. paper)
1. Spiritual life. 2. Self-realization—Religious aspects. I. Title: One hundred and one exercises for the soul. II. Title: One hundred one exercises for the soul. III. Title.
BL624.S533145 2005
204'.46—dc22                                               2005012898

First printing, August 2005
ISBN-10: 1-57731-511-1
ISBN-13: 978-1-57731-511-7
Printed in Canada on acid-free, partially recycled paper

g A proud member of the Green Press Initiative

Distributed to the trade by Publishers Group West

10   9   8   7   6   5   4   3   2   1

---

### Bittersweet
By Dr. Bernie S. Siegel

As we ride our bicycles over the road
She points and says, "Bittersweet."
"What? I can't hear you."
She points again.
I look and see the beauty of Bittersweet;
I feel the peace its beauty brings.

Bittersweet, I am struck by the taste of her words.
They do not make sense,
But they explain our life together
And point out the road to peace.

Bitter, lights left on,
Counter covered with things not put away,
Laundry not folded,
Tired, forgetful, and more.

Sweet, her love, smile, laughter,
Touch, caring, beauty.
Bittersweet, but I hardly taste the bitter
She is so sweet.

Life is Bittersweet
Thank God for you, Honey,
I hope you flavor my life forever.

Do not forget the world is one great family. . . .
Regard Heaven as your father, Earth as your mother,
and all things as your brothers and sisters . . .

— **SHINTO SAYING**

# CONTENTS

❖

# ACKNOWLEDGMENTS

My ever-abiding thanks to all the wonderful teachers in my life, human and otherwise. I would like to thank Andrea Hurst for her dedication and wisdom in helping me to complete this book. Thanks to her associates Christina Lutman, Rachael-Joy Cowham, Jennieke Cohen, Tammy Moon, Mai Tran, John Drehobl, and Sandra Althen for their valuable assistance. My gratitude to the folks at New World Library, Marc Allen, Georgia Hughes, and the other staff who have helped make my books successful.

# INTRODUCTION

Most of us know how important it is to exercise our bodies, but how often do we exercise our souls?

It is easy to get lost in our daily routines and lose touch with the things that are meaningful to us. We become human doings instead of what we are supposed to be — human beings. If this continues, eventually our true self will begin to die. By exercising our souls, however, we enhance our ability to live and love with enthusiasm and vigor, and increase our ability to overcome any difficulties or obstacles we encounter along the way.

Every performer and athlete knows that if you want to get to Carnegie Hall or the Olympics you must practice, practice, practice. If you don't work out regularly, you will never achieve what you are capable of. This is true of the soul as well. And one thing that can help you achieve a gold medal in soul growth is to have a competent coach. It's hard to practice alone. For over thirty years I've counseled people with life-threatening illnesses, and my patients have been my most important teachers and coaches. In this book, let me be your coach. At least, give me a try. I will do my best to encourage you to reach your goals and to help guide you in your soul's journey.

I have written this book in a simple format so that you can sit down anywhere, anytime and find the means to add value to your life. Each chapter focuses on a particular area for soul growth, from improving your attitude to finding inner motivation. Chapters begin with a coaching tip, which introduces the underlying concepts and purpose of the five exercises that follow (exercise 101 is a "final exam"). The exercises are where your workout really begins.

You may find some of the exercises more challenging than others. Feel free to begin anywhere in the book. Consider starting with a chapter that applies to your life right now, one that seems to offer immediate assistance. Begin with the first exercise you are drawn to. No warm-up is needed; you can dive right in. However, since I can't personally be there to remind you to practice every day, try to keep the book in a place where you will see it often and remember to respond to the needs of your soul.

Before you know it you will begin to notice how your life has taken on more meaning and how much better you feel. The change may be small at first, but as we improve ourselves, we make an increasing difference in both our individual lives and the world. The greater our desire and intention, and the more we practice, the greater the results. We can make a positive difference in the world by what we choose to do.

Our body and soul are intended to work together. To accomplish this we must respect our bodies and keep them fit, and we must also understand, respect, and care for that which lies within us. Before you begin, take a moment to look at your soul. What kind of shape is it in? Has it been allowed to express itself — to be exercised properly? Is it underdeveloped in certain places and more developed in others? Imagine that your soul is a muscle that will become stronger, leaner, and more flexible the more you work it. To create a healthy soul, we must first let it speak to us and stop editing it with our fears and our concerns about what others think. We need to trust the divine direction our soul is leading us in and allow it to enhance our life.

Now it is time for you to embark upon your soulful journey.

The Force is with you. Believe me.

Your Coach,
Dr. Bernie S. Siegel

# ATTITUDE IS EVERYTHING

*Don't sweat the small or the large stuff*
*(and save on the cost of deodorant)*

Others can stop you temporarily,
you are the only one who can do it permanently.

— ZIG ZIGLAR

## Coaching Tip One

Maintaining a positive attitude, no matter what your circumstances, increases the likelihood of your finding future happiness and fulfillment. Why is this true? Well, if your attitude is negative and your mind is filled with worry and fear, it takes its toll on your body, mind, and spirit. In fact, by spending all your time creating a vision of an unhappy future, you help create that future. Remember, your thoughts guide your decisions, and negative thoughts lead to negative decisions. Nothing is solved by visualizing the worst outcome, but much can be accomplished when you desire and intend to achieve the best possible result. Optimists may not be more accurate about life — whether interpreting the past or predicting the future — but they live longer than pessimists.

Over God's desk there is a plaque that reads, "If you go around saying I've got a miserable life, I'll show you what miserable really is. And if you go around saying I've got a wonderful life, I'll show you what wonderful really is." A positive attitude can open many doors for you and help create the life you desire.

A negative attitude affects you first by ruining your moment-to-moment happiness. This truth was brought home to me many years ago. One of our children, then aged seven, had an X-ray that revealed a bone tumor. The odds were that it was a malignant tumor and that he would not see another year of life. I was very depressed by what I thought was going to happen, and my attitude showed it. I also tried to get my wife and his four siblings to understand and develop the proper depressing attitude. After all, how can you laugh and play when someone you love is going to die? One day our son walked into the room where I was sitting and said, "Dad, can I talk to you?"

I said, "Sure, what is it?"

He said, "Dad, you're handling this poorly."

With his talk, my son reminded me of what every child and animal knows instinctively: Today is the only day that exists. And as for my son, I was wrong about what was going to happen; he survived and is very much alive and happy today. The future is unknown, and we should never let our fears, worries, and negative attitudes prevent us from enjoying the day and finding fulfillment, no matter what tomorrow seems to hold.

When disappointments and setbacks occur, learn to view them as events that will redirect you to something good. My mother taught me this, and it creates a positive shift in your attitude and your view of the future. Cultivating a hopeful approach to life is an important part of your soul workout. The following exercises, when practiced on a regular basis, will strengthen your outlook and help you to create the life you desire.

## *Exercise 1*

## GRATITUDE LIST

Something to Remember

Why are you living this life? Do you ever stop to think about it? Or are you too busy complaining and whining? Gratitude is one of the best ways to improve your attitude and feel better. You can't be troubled and grateful at the same time. This exercise can be repeated often and will always obtain the same results.

Get a pen and paper and sit down in a quiet place where you won't be interrupted. Start by making a list of at least twenty things you are grateful for in your life. You might start with basic necessities like having a roof over your head, a chair to sit on, food to eat, a warm bed at night, and so on. Then continue with the more meaningful and personal areas of your life, such as your friends, family, work, pets, and health.

When you finish, display the list where you will see it often, especially when troubling thoughts start surfacing. Keep adding to your list over the next several weeks, and take the time every day to read it to remind yourself of all the things in your life you are grateful for.

## *Exercise 2*

## AFFIRMATIONS

What You Say to Yourself Counts

Your intentions and desires shape your future. When you create affirmations about what you desire, and stop visualizing what you fear, your goals are far more likely to manifest themselves. This is because you are preparing yourself and your life for the results you desire.

Take a sheet of paper and draw a vertical line down the middle of the paper. Then take a few minutes to think about all of the major aspects of your life, such as your body, your job, your mate, and so on. Note any negative thoughts, even if they are just momentary, and write them down in the left column. When you've finished your review, read through the negative thoughts you've collected. Now take these thoughts and turn them into positive statements in the right column. For instance:

| | |
|---|---|
| I am very tired today | I feel alive and energized today |
| I wish I didn't have to work today | I look forward to a productive day at work |
| I hate the way my body looks | I am grateful for my body |
| I wish I were a better parent | Every day I'm the best parent I can be |

Post your favorite affirmations where you will see them every day — on your bathroom mirror, on your refrigerator, on your desk, and so on. For thirty days, read them aloud or repeat them silently to yourself several times a day and before bed. Every month re-create your list and choose new affirmations to focus on. As your attitude improves, your body and life will become what you affirm.

## *Exercise 3*
## LEARN FROM A MASTER

Ancient Wisdom

Why should you have to learn the hard way when there are wonderful coaches and teachers who have preceded you? The great sages of the past have left behind words of wisdom to help guide you. Pick up a book by a famous person you admire. Some of the wounded souls, great teachers, and survivors you might consider reading include Helen Keller, Anne Frank, Mother Teresa, Buddha, the Dalai Lama, and St. Francis of Assisi. Take time to read classic poets like Emily Dickinson, Edna St. Vincent Millay, and William Blake.

As you read, keep a notebook of your favorite sayings, quotes, and poems. Or, if you own the book, you might highlight your favorite passages for reference when you need them. Consider framing some of the most uplifting passages and putting them up around your house. When you walk by the framed words of wisdom, let them enlighten you. These teachers and their teachings have inspired millions, and they will act as midwives to help you through the labor pains of self-birthing as you deliver a healthy attitude.

## *Exercise 4*

### THE GREATEST TEACHER

Refuse to Have a Bad Attitude

Recently at a teacher's conference, I asked the audience to tell me who or what they thought was their greatest teacher. There were many answers; some of the most poignant were pain and loss. My answer is death. I refuse to let other people and circumstances impose on my joy, because I know, as we all should, that I have a limited time to live.

I live knowing that for all of us, time on earth is limited. If I hurt others, I make amends, apologize, and move on. If I am feeling fearful, I consider doing what I am afraid of, and if it does not put my life or health at risk, I take a chance.

Our little dog, Furphy, greets dogs ten times his size with a friendly attitude and no fear. He makes many friends, and I am learning from him. Pet training books tell us about the importance of attitude. If you approach another dog with an attitude of fear, your dog will become fearful as well, making conflict more likely. Our attitudes can be detected by those around us, and they affect our inner chemistry as well as the way others treat us.

As an exercise, pretend that the day in front of you is the last day of your life. Savor every moment, even the most mundane. Make the most of every situation. If every day you practice meeting life and the people in it with a positive attitude, then you will be greeted by others with a wagging tail instead of a growl and bared teeth.

## *Exercise 5*

## ADMIRE YOUR BABY PICTURE

Your Divine Inner Child

Fear of failure keeps people from living fully and achieving their greatest potential. This fear does not come from your divine inner child but is learned from those around us. As you grew up, certain authority figures — perhaps your parents, teachers, religious leaders, or others — may have made you feel that, when something went wrong, you were to blame. Rather than address and correct your behavior, they made you feel guilty and shameful for who you were. They were wrong!

You can prove this to yourself quite easily: find one of your baby pictures and a recent picture of yourself. Take some time to look at both photos and notice your attitudes toward them. Most likely, your baby picture will elicit feelings of joy, and any feelings of shame will attach themselves to your adult photo. But what, besides time, is the difference between these two? Carry your baby photo around with you, or display it where you work, and use it as a reminder anytime someone in your life brings up feelings of shame.

You can also take the experiment further, and the next time you see a person in your life who makes you feel bad about yourself, share your baby picture with that person. Notice his or her reaction. Most likely it will be one of adoration, caring comments, and some oohing and aahing. How does this compare to the way the person greets you most of the time?

You still contain within you the divine potential of a child. Others may fail to see it in the adult you have become, but it is there. Do not let a fearful attitude or the opinions of others stop you. Approach life like a child, take the first step, and learn to walk. If you don't try, you won't succeed. If you stumble or fall, like the child, rise and try again.

# GET PHYSICAL

*Develop your strengths —*
*supercharge your workouts*

Movement is a medicine for creating change in a person's
physical, emotional, and mental states.

— **CAROL WELCH**

## Coaching Tip Two

If we listen, our bodies have a great deal of valuable
information to share with us. Our bodies can teach us
about ourselves. We are born as physical beings, and yet
the older we get the more we tend to ignore the wisdom
of our bodies. In order to improve the health of our
souls, we must learn to pay attention to our physical self.
We must remain in touch with our bodies in order to
have direct access to all the valuable information they
can communicate.

As a physician, I know our very lives are stored within
us. We need to learn how to interpret our body's language.

The body can speak to us through more than physical symptoms like pain. The body affects our thoughts, dreams, and feelings. I have used the intuitive wisdom of the body, expressed by people in their dreams and drawings, to help them make therapeutic decisions and to diagnose illnesses. This knowledge is not taught in medical schools, but it has been known for many decades through the work of Carl Jung.

This works both ways, for the body is affected by the images we present it with. For instance, picture a pleasant event or scene and notice how your body reacts — as if you were really experiencing it. We know that an actor's immune system and cortisol levels are altered by the roles he or she plays. Acting in a comedy enhances immune function and lowers stress hormone levels, while performing in a tragedy has a detrimental physical effect. The body does not distinguish between emotions felt when performing a role or those experienced during an actual event. Both have an effect.

Pleasant physical activities — like petting a dog or getting a massage — enhance certain hormone levels that have the beneficial effect of making us feel more at peace and loving toward one another. We were born to be touched and to touch others. That is what our bodies are for. They allow us to express ourselves through touch, movement, speech, and displays of affection.

Your heart knows you better than your head. Listen to what it tells you and keep in touch with the messages your body is sending you. The exercises in this chapter will help you use your body to improve the health of your soul.

## *Exercise* 6

## GET A MASSAGE

Release Stress

Massage can be very therapeutic because, when you are touched, your body chemistry is altered in a positive way. This includes factors that suppress pain and that stimulate growth and your immune system.

For this exercise, get a massage. Consider getting one several times a week or once a week for a month, and notice its effect on you. Either find a massage therapist or ask someone close to you to give it a try. Use scented oils and play relaxing music. While being massaged, allow your mind to go wherever it desires; connect with the emotions that come up as you are touched and spend some time exploring them within your journal or with someone you trust. Therapeutic massage can be a tool to help you return to normal and healthy physical relationships.

Remember to give those you care about a massage, too. Any activity that increases human contact is soothing. It can be something as simple as rubbing someone's neck and shoulders. Giving yourself a good foot massage now and then is also highly recommended.

## *Exercise 7*

# PET A FURRY ANIMAL

### Soft and Warm

There have been many studies showing the benefits of having pets and spending time with them. Just as human contact changes your hormone levels, you can lower your blood pressure and improve your mood by petting an animal.

If you have a pet, spend time with it every day, gently stroking it and sending it loving thoughts. Get to know each other through touch and play. Animals are very intuitive and can help you to know yourself and to learn to improve your own intuitiveness and nonverbal communication. If you don't have a pet, consider getting one. Any type of animal will do, so long as you can relate to it and feel comfortable sharing your affection with it — if you're not a dog person, why not a cat, bird, fish, reptile, or other animal? Reap the benefits of a meaningful relationship with a pet. For more, see chapter 11.

If you don't have a pet and can't keep one in your home, visit a local animal shelter and spend time with the animals there; they are always eager for company. Take a dog for a walk or hold a bunch of kittens in your arms. Last, if you cannot find a warm-blooded animal — start with a cuddly teddy bear and work your way up.

# Exercise *8*

## TAKE A WALK

Eyes Open, Eyes Closed

When we move our body, we create an internal environment that every physician in every specialty would verify is therapeutic. When we walk, we get a chance to listen to ourselves and hear our inner voice.

So get away from distractions and take yourself for a walk in nature. It is a wonderful way to get in touch with the earth we live on. Try three different types of walks; each one should last at least an hour. First, go alone with no distractions. Take the time to see the beauty around you and to listen to your own thoughts; notice the feelings that arise in your body. Focus on your physical environment — the variety of shapes and colors and the effect of the breeze on plants and trees. Stop and look at the weeds and the beautiful little flowers they contain. Give yourself time to be, and notice how your view of life and nature changes when you learn to truly see what is before you. For the second walk, take the same approach and do the same things, only bring your pet with you this time and notice what attracts it.

For the third walk, find a friend or family member you trust and ask the person to join you on a walk in a park or the woods. Have the person put a blindfold on you and guide you to trees and flowers so you can feel, smell, and experience them without sight. Note how alert all your senses become and what you learn about the physical world on this walk.

## *Exercise 9*

## GO TO THE GYM

### Be in Training

Regular exercise has many benefits — ranging from boosting the immune system to reducing stress, increasing mental alertness, producing antidepressants and anti-aging effects, and more. Whether your workout consists of weights, aerobics, or another form of movement, it is all beneficial. And that is the goal of this exercise: developing a regular workout routine.

Find a place where you feel comfortable exercising. This could be in your home, in a local park, or in a public or private gym. Consider all your options; which environment will support your efforts best? Will you be fine on your own, or do you need the commitment of a class to keep you on track? Some private gyms are casual, while some are very high tech, high pressure, and expensive. Which fits you best? You need a place where you will feel comfortable and where you can proceed with your routine without interruptions.

Start with a simple exercise plan and build up slowly. This might mean beginning with just twenty or thirty minutes of jogging on a treadmill or lifting weights. For some, a personal trainer may be helpful in developing an appropriate routine. Awaken your body slowly to how it feels to move and exercise as it learns what it is capable of. Don't try to get fit overnight. Give yourself time to train and develop, and after every session, take a moment to feel proud of what you are accomplishing.

## *Exercise 10*

# TRY SOMETHING NEW

Earth, Air, or Sea

A great way to get in touch with your body and move beyond your fears, inherited or acquired, is to do something you have not tried before. This requires courage and gives you a whole new set of sensations to contemplate; it makes you feel alive. For this exercise, choose three activities you've always wanted to try, or haven't done since you were a kid, and do them.

Think about the things you enjoyed as a child, such as jumping rope, playing tetherball, swimming, roller-skating, riding your bike, or playing ball. Which did you love but gave up when you got "too old" for it? Is there a sport or game you always wish you'd gotten really good at, but never pursued? Be a kid again and take a chance. Or tackle some activity that only appeals to you now: learn how to salsa dance, skydive, scuba dive, bungee jump, rock climb, surf, or shoot pool. Take a lesson or class if you have to. Even if you just ride a roller coaster, give your body a thrill. Let your body know you love the experience and sensations of life.

# HUMOR WILL HELP YOU FINISH

3

*...no matter what race you enter*

And we should consider every day lost on which we have not danced at least once. And we should call every truth false which was not accompanied by at least one laugh.

— **FRIEDRICH NIETZSCHE**

## Coaching Tip Three

As we get older, it is important to maintain a childlike sense of humor and to let your inner child express itself; otherwise, life can become oppressive and difficult. I know from experience how easy it is to focus on what is troubling me rather than on what heals and sustains me. Our souls are light, and we must be willing to see the light side of life and to encourage laughter on a daily basis.

When we are children, humor comes naturally. As adults, it can take effort to inject humor into our lives. I have tried to cultivate a childlike perspective when I am out in the world, seeing things as if through the eyes of a child. I follow directions exactly as they are given. When I am asked to "sign here," I write "here" on the slip. That keeps things light and in perspective. When I buy lottery tickets, I always ask the woman selling them if she will marry me if I win. Some of the answers have been very interesting! I also ask for senior discounts no matter what day they are offered, telling the clerks that seniors can't remember what day it is anyway, so I want my discount.

It takes courage to be a clown. One must have self-esteem and not worry about what others think of you. Another example is the mailbox at the bottom of our driveway, which is fifteen feet in the air. Painted on the side are the words "Air Mail." Everyone knows our house at the post office. Most of all, when you act like a clown, you meet and encourage the clown in others; you discover children of all ages. I once entered an area that said, "Nobody allowed here," saying to the guard, "I am a nobody." The guard earned my respect and a hug by telling me he was making me a "somebody" — and so I had to leave.

One time I even dressed as a nurse at a surgical department dinner. I wore a white nurse's outfit I borrowed from our office staff, plus balloons for breasts, a wig, and makeup applied by my wife. And like Dustin Hoffman in *Tootsie*, I got up and gave a critical, impassioned speech. I was amazed by the positive comments I received the next day at the hospital. Humor makes everything easier to digest.

It is wonderful when your ability to laugh brings out the child in another person; you both then experience a much better day. At my post office recently, the clerk told me some jokes while he processed my package. I told him I was going to mail empty boxes just to come in and hear his jokes.

Humor helps us get through even the toughest of times. The exercises in this chapter will supply you with ideas and sources to bring humor back into your daily life and uplift your soul.

## *Exercise 11*

## KEEP A SMILE JOURNAL

### Humor in Your Daily Life

Throughout my life, my tendency has been to make notes about painful events, and not the humorous and healing ones. I had to learn to become aware of the latter events. In this way, what is stored within me are not just the hard times but the joyful ones. In general, I suggest you always make notes to keep yourself consciously aware of the meaningful moments in your life.

For the next week, however, do something more specific. Carry a small journal, and every time you find yourself smiling or laughing, pause to write down the details of the moment. Write descriptions of the events that make you smile, from emails to chance encounters in the supermarket. Read your pages every evening before you go to bed, and in the morning reread your notes to prepare yourself for another joyful day.

Notice what type of humor appeals to you and inspires your childlike laughter. Keep this journal as a resource so you can refer to it when the clouds block the sunshine out of your life. You will discover you can make your own weather.

## *Exercise 12*

## SHARE A FUNNY STORY

History and Laughter

When you laugh, you transcend the physical aspects of your life and your troubles. Humorous stories shared with family and friends are a great way to bond with others while having a great time.

For this exercise, accumulate material in your life that makes you laugh and share it with your loved ones. If you are not sure how to begin, schedule a family dinner and an evening around sharing stories, old photos, and videos. This will bring you all closer, heal wounds, and help you to smile at the past.

Ask friends and especially senior relatives to share memories. To get a storytelling session rolling, you need only ask them questions about old times. Believe me, you will soon find yourself immersed in humor and love.

## *Exercise 13*

# WATCH A COMEDY

### Laugh Together

It's true — laughter is the best medicine. In his book *Anatomy of an Illness*, Norman Cousins demonstrated a positive therapeutic response to watching *Candid Camera* videos. Studies reveal that just anticipating seeing a comedy changes people's internal chemistry.

This exercise couldn't be easier. Set aside an evening to watch a funny movie at home with your family and friends and just enjoy some laughter together. Those are the moments in life that we always treasure. Now, don't fight over which movie you choose: follow my prescription of an initial dose of Mel Brooks with a booster shot of Woody Allen. Or, treat everyone to a movie in the theater and make a point afterward to spend some time together retelling the jokes and reliving the scenes that you enjoyed the most.

Your world is not likely to experience a disaster because you weren't serious for every minute of your life, and it may well avoid one because humor heals wounds. Who can get angry at a clown? So kick back and find something that makes you laugh!

On a side note, if you want to enjoy a car trip with the family, bring along a CD or tape of Mel Brooks's *2000 Year Old Man* with Carl Reiner and play it as you drive. Just keep your eyes on the road as you laugh.

## Exercise *14*

### READ THE COMICS

Laugh through the Week

Here's another easy exercise: take time to read the comics. This is worthwhile not just because they will make you laugh but because they contain wisdom about the nature of life. Charlie Brown and Blondie are part of my morning ritual and help me to start the day with a knowing smile.

Next time you read the comics section of the newspaper, cut out a cartoon that makes you laugh. Post it wherever you need it most, such as on your refrigerator, a bulletin board, or at work — so that every time you see it, you will smile and feel your spirit lifted. Share your favorites with your friends and family so that everyone can get a good laugh, too.

Take your comics with you when you go to visit sick friends who can really use a good laugh. And don't forget your doctor, too.

## *Exercise 15*

# DO THE UNEXPECTED

### Make People Laugh

If you can bring variety and childlike humor to the everyday situations in your life, it will definitely make your life more interesting. For instance, when I go to Ernie's Pizza to pick up an order, I always ask if my Chinese food is ready. The boss knows me and laughs, but his staff always tells me I am in the wrong restaurant and tries to help me figure out where I should be. Well, guess what was waiting for me the last time I went to pick up our pizza? Right! Three containers of Chinese food, and the whole restaurant was in an uproar.

Love and humor benefit both the giver and the receiver. Creating a situation that makes others laugh lifts everyone's spirits. Finding ways to do the opposite of what people normally expect keeps life from getting drab and dreary. Playing the trickster is good for the soul.

So keep the child in you alive, and for this exercise do three unexpected things. These could be small things — like sitting down with your child to draw and coloring only outside the lines or throwing a dinner party and serving breakfast. Be creative. The street where I live is a dead end, and on the sign that says "no outlet" I hung one that says "bring batteries." Do what Bernie would do: get a kick out of your day and bring out the child in everyone.

CHAPTER

# VOCAL WARM-UPS

*Find your voice and sing your song*

When we have the courage to speak out — to break our
silence — we inspire the rest of the "moderates" in our
communities to speak up and voice their views.

— SHARON SCHUSTER

## Coaching Tip Four

Sometimes one of the most difficult things to do is to
speak up and say what we are thinking and feeling. We
are brought up with so many voices telling us what to
think, what to say, and what to do that often it is hard
even to hear our own inner voice.

So we bury our feelings instead of finding our voice,
speaking about our needs, and sharing the truth about
how we feel with those who ask and truly care. We lose
the ability to connect with others. You may not want to tell
strangers in the supermarket how you really feel when
they ask, "How are you?" But you are not obligated to

hide your truth either, and only with honesty are we likely to start a meaningful conversation.

I recently asked a roomful of nine-year-olds, "How are you?" I got twenty-one "Good" or "Fine" answers. Then I asked, "Is that really true?" All of their heads shook no. We are taught very early in life to edit ourselves for others, but if you want to live a healthy and fulfilling adult life, you need to find your voice and speak your truth. It is okay to be a scurvy elephant. That's what one child thought the teacher had called him. Turns out he was speaking up and then being labeled a "disturbing element."

In order to speak our truth we first need to be able to distinguish our own voice from that of the voices of authority that reside in our head. What voices from your past keep speaking to you? Do these voices help or hinder you? If they don't help, you can stop listening. It's up to you. You can edit or censor their comments, and by finding your own true inner voice, you can forever silence these negative voices. To do this, you must accept yourself and believe in your own intrinsic value and divine nature.

The exercises in this chapter will help you to access your voice and strengthen your resolve to use it in a healthy and empowering fashion.

## *Exercise 16*

### ROLE PLAYING

Play the Part You Admire

If you could be an actor or actress in any play or movie, what character would you most like to portray? Would you want to be Queen Guinevere in *Camelot* or Eva Peron in *Evita*? Tevye in *Fiddler on the Roof* or Felix in *The Odd Couple*? For this exercise, choose a character whose actions and attributes you admire, and for one week try to emulate the character as much as possible. Ask yourself how the character would act if faced with the situations in your daily life, and then play that part. Make sure to see the movie or read the play so that the character is fresh in your mind.

For instance, what would your character do at your job when a decision needs to be made? How would the character handle an argument with a spouse or keep from feeling down? Notice how this changes your inter-actions with others and how you perceive yourself in and out of character. When you are done performing at the end of the week, continue to incorporate the charac-teristics you like best into your own personality. And if in playing a character you act too "out of character" — remember, don't judge yourself too harshly. This is about rehearsing and practicing until you become the person you want to be.

## *Exercise 17*

# PRACTICE SAYING NO

### Setting Limits

In our efforts to be the good child, the perfect spouse, the uncomplaining employee, or the cooperative patient, many of us fall into the trap of trying to appease people by going along with whatever they want us to do. At times we lose track of our own boundaries and needs, and the cost of this could be our life, both symbolically and literally. When we are unable to set healthy limits, it causes distress in our relationships. But when we learn to say no in order to say yes to our true self, we feel empowered and our relationships with others improve.

For this exercise, take a look at your life and see if there are any times when you say yes even though you want to say no. Have you fallen into unspoken agreements at home or at work that you wish to change? Choose one, and for one week, say no to it. For one week, when someone asks you for a favor, don't respond immediately. Tell the person you need to think about it, then take the time to decide if you really *want* to do it or not. If not, say no, even if this seems impolite. Why? Because you are rehearsing survival behavior. A woman I know who has cancer always says no to whatever her doctor recommends. He then stops to explain things to her and truly communicate what he feels is best for her. She ends up doing most of the things he tells her, but she also gains the information she needs to feel empowered in her treatment. For this exercise, at the end of one week, evaluate which of your new boundaries you want to maintain and which you might relax.

But don't be afraid to keep saying no. Try to catch yourself in the moment and use your true voice to say what you really want to say: NO! Stop nursing others and start mothering yourself.

# Exercise *18*

## MAKE MUSIC

### Sing a Song

My mother-in-law was an opera singer, and while waiting to take her daughter out, I would sit at her piano and sing off-key; it was torture for her. After many years of coaching by her and her daughter, who is now my wife, I have finally learned how to sing. The other day my wife fell asleep while we were on a long drive, and I started singing to myself. Before she opened her eyes, she said, "Is the radio on?" That is the greatest compliment I have ever received.

For this exercise, start singing whenever you get the chance, but make a point of it for at least one week. Sing the song "My Way," but do it your way and be heard. Music and singing are very healing to the spirit. The rhythm of music puts us more in touch with our environment, and performing music teaches us to be more expressive in all aspects of our lives. Create your tune, compose your lyrics, buy a drum, and turn your life into a song. We will be the chorus that accompanies you.

If you want to go a step further, take singing lessons. But even if you don't take lessons, set time aside each day to sing. If, like me, you are not naturally gifted, give your family a break and use the shower or sing when you are alone in the car. After all, it has taken many years for my wife to enjoy my singing.

# *Exercise 19*
## EXPRESS YOURSELF

### Learn to Growl

Another way we stifle our true voice is by keeping a lid on our feelings, but doing this hurts us emotionally and physically. We need to be able to express how we feel and to ask for what we need. Think of something that you want to ask for, or words that you need to share that you have never spoken. What is the worst thing that could happen if you had the courage to speak? How people respond is up to them. But only you are responsible for expressing yourself.

Anger can be the hardest emotion to express, especially for women. If you are treated with disrespect, it is appropriate to express your anger; that is survival behavior. In nature this is expected. Many years ago, a poisonous snake was threatening to bite our children while they were playing outside. I went and I asked it to please not bite the children. A week later I went to thank the snake for not biting our children. He was covered with bruises. I asked what happened. He said, "Your kids aren't afraid of me anymore, and so they run all over me while they are playing."

I said, "I asked you not to bite. I didn't say you couldn't hiss."

For this exercise, take that lesson to heart. Practice your growl and hiss. Start by growling at yourself in the mirror. Express those feelings. At first, do so alone, but then, if it's appropriate, share those feelings with the person to which they are directed. If it involves family, tell them what you are doing, and remember that anger over a person's behavior and love for that person can coexist.

## *Exercise 20*

### GIVE A SPEECH

#### Be Heard

There is no reason to have a voice unless you are going to use it. God wouldn't have created so many noisy creatures if they weren't supposed to use their voices. Children and animals know that when you want something, you make noise.

As you get to know your voice through the exercises in this chapter, start using it to speak out. For this exercise, give a speech and share your ideas with others. Speaking out can be one of the hardest things to do because of how most of us were brought up. Parents and teachers told us to be quiet and not disturb anyone. Most people fear speaking out, and giving a speech can create panic, but it is a great way to be heard and gain confidence in yourself and your voice.

Find a group like Toastmasters, or enroll in a speech class, or ask to give a talk for an organization like the PTA. If all else fails, prepare a speech and give it to your family and friends. Prepare a talk on a subject you know well. Then share all the wonderful things you have to say and notice how freeing that can be.

# TEAM SPIRIT

*Create your team and participate in the World Series of life*

Coming together is a beginning.
Keeping together is progress.
Working together is success.

— HENRY FORD

## Coaching Tip Five

Humans, by their nature, are social beings; they need support and interaction with other people on their journey through life. When you encourage others, it rewards both the giver and the receiver and creates a circle of support that you can count on during tough times. Those who have experienced that kind of support and love from their family and friends are fortunate. Others may have never experienced this, or felt it only sporadically. However, all of us need to practice our teamwork. When it's game time, we need to know every position is covered and everyone knows how to play together.

Who is on your team? Do you need more players? Are you showing up for other team members when they are troubled? A team needs to work together for the common good. Each member must be willing to listen to the others and be available in times of need. It can be easy to become self-involved and forget that others are relying on us as much as we are relying on them. Open up to friends and family about your life, and listen to them about theirs, and you will increase your mutual understanding and intimacy while building team spirit.

The exercises in this chapter will help you to attract members to build a successful team for support in your life.

## Exercise *21*

### SCRAPBOOKING

Putting the Pieces Together

Taking stock of our past is as important as taking stock of our present, and one great way to do this is to create a scrapbook. This process can be both emotional and insightful, particularly when our intention is to celebrate and remember the team that got us to where we are today. Once finished, your scrapbook will also become a keepsake for future generations.

Go to a craft store and purchase an album with a meaningful cover, and buy any other items you may need for your project, such as stickers and specialty papers. Start by pulling out all your old boxes of photos and keepsakes. Open up all the drawers and containers that have been sitting around forever. This may seem daunting at first, but believe me, it will not be work once you start. As you go through the items, you will relive your history and the story of your life. These are a part of your immortality, too.

Organize your scrapbook any way you like; proceed through time or sort people and events by topics, such as weddings, birthdays, vacations, best friends, sports, awards, and so on. As you paste items and photos into the scrapbook, add special captions so that anyone, including future family members, can appreciate the book in years to come. Make notes on the pages with comments, details, memories, and anything else you want to share. We have done this for all of our children so they will know their ancestors.

As you put the scrapbook together, make a point to relive all the experiences you are documenting with the family, friends, acquaintances, pets, and other people who have supported and cheered you on through all your life events. Then, of course, when you have completed the album, share it with those you love. Laugh at what used to bother you, and treasure the love you find still present in the memories.

## *Exercise 22*

## POTLUCK

### Have a Party

A great way to assemble your circle of friends and family is to have a party. For a change of pace, make it a surprise party. Invite everyone but don't tell them why. When they arrive, they'll be pleasantly surprised to find they are being celebrated, rather than the host, and they can have a good time with no expectations.

An even better way to build your team of family and friends is to create a regular potluck event. Rotate locations, and make it where the host does not prepare anything, but the guests bring all that is needed. Potlucks allow guests to display their creativity and make a special and meaningful contribution.

At your party, when everyone is relaxed and enjoying themselves, suggest sharing stories of the past about each other. You can bring out old photo albums and videos that include the people attending. As you share the collection, tell the stories behind them and ask each friend and family member to share his or her stories as well. If possible, make copies for people to take home as gifts and watch again at their own leisure, to enjoy their everlasting connections. Over time, make a record of the stories that are told; this can be a great take-home gift as well. Guests may have come together for potluck, but the flavor of the end result is very special.

## *Exercise 23*

## MAKE A FRIEND

The More, the Merrier

Friends are an important part of your team, and you can never have enough. The next time you are hosting a special event or celebrating a holiday, ask a neighbor or a coworker you do not know well to share the festivities with you. If you have the courage, go beyond that and host an event for and/or invite people in need, so they can have a day of joy and a nice meal, too. When you feel comfortable, give everyone you invite the opportunity to share what they are grateful for in their life.

And here is another challenging thought — invite an enemy. Kindness is a powerful weapon that can turn enemies into friends. Even if the person doesn't want to come, the invitation itself may create a change in your relationship. Hit them with a powerful weapon — kindness.

We forget that even a small act of kindness makes a difference. So smile at your neighbor whenever you meet and set a date for your next party.

## *Exercise 24*

## GIVING BACK

Get Involved in Your Community

What is community? For me, community is everything that exists on this planet. We all need each other to survive. The Creator certainly made it a bit complicated, but it sure is interesting this way. I can't answer every question about why we need certain insects, snakes, fish, people, and so on, but we all seem necessary. All our actions and their effects are interconnected. You are part of the greater community, too. There are no exceptions.

For this exercise, your assignment is to contribute something to the wider community — whether that's your city, state, country, or the world. Join a recycling program or a community outreach program. Work with children and teach them to respect the community that is this planet.

If possible, be involved financially. Donate to meaningful charities of your choice — if not with money, then with your time and skills. With each decision you make, ask yourself, "Is what I am doing good not only for myself but for my community?"

Ultimately, one of the best ways for you to get involved is to get elected to local public office. Then you will be helping directly to make the decisions that are best for your community, for today and tomorrow.

*Exercise 25*

## JOIN A SUPPORT GROUP

Be Supported

People have a very basic problem...they worry. They wonder about what will happen tomorrow, and they visualize the worst-case scenarios. Then they need support to deal with their fears and worries, many of which will never happen — but that's irrelevant when they are worrying about what they think will happen.

What do you worry about? For this exercise, join or create a support group that deals with the topic. If you decide to create your own, enlist family and friends who share your concerns, and meet once a week. Make up your own local "Worriers Anonymous" chapter; people will love it.

Why is a support group, be it of your biological family or of others, helpful? The answer is because the natives know how to help each other. When you are living through something difficult, you don't want advice and so-called help from tourists who have no clue about what you are feeling. Powerful events are not experienced intellectually, like reading a diagnosis or description of a disaster; they are emotional experiences unique to the participants. Support groups are collections of empathetic, nonjudgmental people who try to help one another get through a similar experience. A support group will listen to your story and share their own so you can become wiser and not have to solve everything yourself.

One word of warning — some groups and individuals seem to enjoy their troubles because they bring them attention. If you find yourself in a "victim group," don't return; just find another one that focuses on love and healing.

# COMING FROM YOUR HEART

*Do the things you love*

To love what you do and feel that it matters —
how could anything be more fun?

— **KATHARINE GRAHAM**

## Coaching Tip Six

Your heart, not your head, should decide how you spend your life. You were created to do the things you love. When your heart is full and joyful, it is reflected in the health of your body, mind, and spirit. Your life will be more fulfilling when you make choices that come from your heart.

When you do what you love in a job or career, it never seems like you are working. How many of us feel this way? Mondays have a higher illness and mortality rate than other days of the week, and that's because many people are working at jobs they don't enjoy just to make a living. Some follow particular careers because they feel they are supposed to, or they are trying to earn more than the next guy. As Joseph Campbell warned, "You climb the ladder of success, and when you get to the top it's leaning against the wrong wall."

One time a physician friend of mine asked me to read an article she had written that discussed the type of people who were more apt to survive traumatic events that most others could not. What struck me was how those who shared love were most likely to survive, and after reading her piece I told her I thought the idea of a "love gene" was wonderful. She said she had not written about a love gene but a "survival gene," but she enjoyed my perspective. The idea of a love gene makes sense, since when we do what we love we change our physiology and can create miracles.

Sometimes it takes a life crisis to start listening to what our heart is telling us. I have seen people who, when told they have a short time to live, stop doing what they don't want to do and begin to do what feels right. One person I know was once told he had a few months to live, and so he moved to the mountains of Colorado. When I wasn't contacted to attend his funeral, I called his wife. Instead, the man answered the phone and said, "It is so beautiful here, I forgot to die."

So do what you love. You may become physically tired, but you will never become tired of your life! When you eliminate the life that is killing you, you save your true life.

# Exercise 26

## COOK UP A DISH

### Nourish Yourself

Some people love to cook, while others see it as work — so for some this exercise will come easily, and for others it will be more of a challenge. Since we all need to eat, why not make something that nourishes our hearts and souls as well as our bodies?

I think cooking is a very creative art form, and I admire people who are good at it. I am currently learning from some talented performers. It is such a gift to create a meal that brings both joy and nourishment, and that is your goal for this exercise. Find a recipe that excites your tastes and talents, and then prepare it for your family and friends. Make it a special occasion: eat in the dining room, use your fine china, burn incense or aromatic candles, play music, and do anything else that will make the event special.

But don't create extra pressure for yourself. If you are not a comfortable cook, plan for a simple meal. Make the actual preparation of the meal a relaxing, enjoyable activity. Be prepared, and don't feel rushed. Have snacks waiting for when your guests arrive. Allow yourself the time to truly enjoy your creation. When a meal comes out of the oven of love, everyone is nourished. Remember, what your recipe of life consists of is up to you.

*Exercise 27*

## STARLIGHT, CANDLELIGHT

Peace and Reflection

As I write this, my home is filled with electricians try-ing to find out why our main circuit breaker keeps pop-ping and leaving us in darkness. Maybe our creator is telling me that it's time to take a break and sit quietly in the candlelight or outside in the moonlight. I can enjoy the peace and look up at the stars. In fact, too much time under artificial light can create stress.

When my mother lost her sight, one of the resulting gifts was that she couldn't see the house and whether it was dirty or not when guests arrived. It made her life easier because she didn't have to worry about cleaning all of the time.

Tonight, turn off the lights. Sit outside under the stars and bathe in the light of creation. If the weather has other ideas, sit quietly in the darkness of your home and light candles or a fire to warm you and restore your energy. Contemplate the ways you artificially create stress in your life and pledge to change those things. Just as you can restore light to your home by resetting the circuit breaker, you can restore it to your life by resetting your desires, expectations, and sense of gratitude.

# Exercise 28

## CREATE A GAME

### Find Out What You Love

When you use creative approaches to learn more about yourself, you receive many new insights and revelations. In this exercise you will make a board game out of your own life to discover some of the things you love to do.

On a large piece of cardboard, draw squares around the perimeter, as in Monopoly. In the squares, write meaningful past events and possible future events or dreams you have for your life. Leave a handful of squares blank. Let your thoughts and feelings go as you consider what to write and include every possible option.

Next, take about twenty or thirty blank index cards and write on them a series of actions or activities: those things that you love to do, those that support you, those that drain you, those you never want to do, and so on. If you have trouble thinking of any, refer back to things that you liked and didn't like to do as a child. As in Monopoly, select some small household item to be the game piece that represents you — choose a positive symbol. Then roll a pair of dice and start to move through the game of your life. If you land on a blank square, turn over a card and read what you are to do.

This is your life. Play the game and remember you are here to play and do what you love. It is not about winning or losing; it is about living and experiencing the game. You are a winner just by showing up.

## *Exercise 29*

# LET YOUR HEART DECIDE

Questions & Answers

Sometimes we get into a rut and find ourselves constantly tired or depressed, so that even taking time off or resting doesn't seem to change the way we feel. The reason is that we have stopped paying attention to our feelings and are no longer listening to our heart. Our inner child wants to be heard and do what makes it happy; it wants to burn up its energy and not burn out.

For this exercise, you will need to meditate. Find a quiet place where you will not be disturbed so you can relax and listen to your inner voice. When comfortable, begin by taking deep breaths; focus on the motion of your chest and completely relax. Ask these questions of your heart: What do you love to do? What do you want to do today? Now open your treasure chest and listen to the answers.

Be open to whatever your feelings tell you. If you need help to accomplish what your heart tells you to do, ask for spiritual direction, too. Your answers will be revealed by how your heart feels, not what your mind thinks. It may tell you things that surprise you, so be ready to begin the journey of transformation.

## *Exercise 30*

### TAKE A QUIZ

Do You Love What You Do?

Do you love your job, or does it bore you? Do you hate to get out of bed every day? Do you feel tired even when you haven't done anything strenuous? Do you rarely find anything to smile or laugh about? Do you need caffeine to keep you going? Here is a short quiz to help you focus your thinking.

On a scale of 1 to 5, answer these questions regarding your job:

1=Never  2=Occasionally  3=Sometimes
4=Often  5=Always

1. Do you have trouble staying focused or does your mind wander while you are at work?
   1          2          3          4          5

2. When you come home from work, do you feel as though you haven't accomplished anything?
   1          2          3          4          5

3. How often do you think about all of the other things you could be doing while you are at work?
   1          2          3          4          5

4. Do you fantasize about leaving your job and embarking on an exciting new career?

   1          2          3          4          5

5. Do you wish you had a different boss, coworkers, clients, or customers?

   1          2          3          4          5

6. Do you feel you are not being acknowledged and praised for your work?

   1          2          3          4          5

7. At the end of the day do you feel your work lacks meaning?

   1          2          3          4          5

Review your answers. If most of your scores are fours and fives, you have two choices. You can either change your attitude or your job. To change your attitude, you have to begin to see the people you work with differently. Get to know them and their lives, find ways to serve and help them, and you will feel rewarded by your efforts at work.

If you want a new job, then sit down and make a list of the things you love to do. Then ask yourself, "How can I incorporate these activities into a career?" For example: If you love to write, start writing a novel or poetry, or your life story. Or go to your local newspaper and see if you can contribute freelance articles. Volunteer to try out the jobs you might want to do. If you love animals, help out at the local shelter. Once you have explored these other avenues, take steps to follow your heart and find the work you love. This could lead to going to veterinary school, becoming an animal control officer, or creating a sanctuary for animal rescue.

# MOVE INTO THE SUNSHINE

*Nature as nurture*

Climb the mountains and get their good tidings.
Nature's peace will flow into you as sunshine flows
into trees. The winds will blow their own freshness into
you and the storms their energy, while cares will drop
away from you like the leaves of autumn.

— JOHN MUIR

## Coaching Tip Seven

Nature is always available, easily accessible, and one of
the best ways to seek inner healing. Whenever you are
feeling stressed, confused, or down, go outside and ask
nature to give you an answer to your problems. Then
listen and observe the water, wind, birds, animals, and
more. You will notice how much better you feel when
nature answers you.

Most of the time we are forced to listen to the noise
of society: horns, engines, and sirens. We do not even
realize how much these sounds can affect us in a negative way. Which sounds bring you peace and which

create anxiety? When your soul needs exercise, nature is its gym.

As often as possible, let the harmony of nature surround you and bring peace to all of your senses. Observing nature helps you to heal and stay calm, when you are caught in traffic, stuck in a hospital room or an office, or working alone at home. If you can see nature through your window, any situation will be less stressful and you will cope better.

Stay in touch with Mother Nature. Spend time outside in the sunshine, and have faith that, no matter what your circumstances, you will be a survivor.

# Exercise 31

## NATURE POEM

### Celebrating the World Around You

Writing a poem about the beauty around you is a wonderful way to celebrate your feelings, observations, and gratitude for nature's abundance. You can also learn to value yourself more through the appreciation of the natural world.

Pack up a journal, notebook, or specially designed paper; grab a favorite pen or pencil. Then spend time alone walking through a park, along the beach, or even in your backyard. Observe and listen to the beauty and tranquillity that surrounds you. As you walk, make mental and written notes about what you are seeing and how it is affecting you. I can recall once when a fawn crossed my path how it intensified my awareness of the beauty of nature.

Once you have spent time exploring the area, find a favorite spot to sit down and write some descriptions of the world you see around you. Try to come up with original ways to talk about the ocean, a tree, flower, or bird. Next, begin to create a poem. I call it poetry, but it doesn't have to rhyme. Explore and express your vision and new awareness.

Let the words flow without thought or judgment.

This is a wonderful way to bond with nature and truly begin to see what is before you. Share your vision of beauty with others and reread your poems when you find yourself feeling depleted. Nature's wonder will restore you to life.

*Exercise 32*

## GARDENING

Get Your Hands in the Dirt

I find gardening to be a great way to submerge myself in nature and become a cocreator. Setting aside time to be outdoors and work with the earth is one of the most rewarding activities I can think of. Being surrounded by nature brings me a sense of peace and reawakens my spirit.

For this exercise, plant a garden of vegetables or flowers. Keep the garden small so it will not become a daunting project, and tend to it every day. City dwellers can plant window boxes or create "gardens" of potted plants indoors.

Whenever I garden I think of what I am putting back into the earth that will be experienced by those who come after me. Through my acts of creation, life will continue to exist and grow. I do not hire anyone to mow my lawn because I love to find baby trees and then preserve or replant them. When I preserve beauty for the world to experience, I receive a gift every day. Each year I watch the trees grow and blossom, just as I watched our children as they grew up. When I do these small acts, I feel as though I am part of something bigger and am connected to all living things.

Think of yourself and the important people in your life as if you were flowers or trees. How can you encourage your growth? What nourishes you and gives you and those you love strong roots to grow from and branches that are not afraid to reach for the sky?

## *Exercise 33*
### PLANTS, AROMAS, AND PETS

Bring Nature into Your Home

A shelter is something that humans created to protect themselves from the dangers inherent in nature. But our modern shelters also separate us from nature, and it is time that we put nature back into our homes. When we isolate ourselves from the world around us, we feel separated from life and become more prone to disease and unable to handle stress. Our homes and our communities are filled with depersonalizing electronic devices.

Nature is vital to our health and happiness. My home is filled with plants that I water and animals that I take care of. They give my life meaning and connect me with nature. Plants also purify the air and are calming to look at, while appropriate aromas create a sense of tranquillity.

For this exercise, buy plants for your home and office, and take the time to care for them. Consider adopting a pet. Add some calming aromas, perhaps from childhood memories, to your environment. You will feel happier and healthier when nature is inside and outside your home.

## Exercise *34*

## POND REFLECTION

The Soothing Effects of Water

Finding serenity in our lives is never easy. We are always on the go, moving from activity to activity and keeping long lists of tasks that need to be accomplished. Nature, on the other hand, has seasons but no schedule. It is the primary source of beauty and tranquillity that can calm and pacify your soul.

When I visit Hawaii, the mountains, ocean, blue sky, beautiful plants, and God's symbol — the rainbow — leave me in awe and wonder. For this exercise, take a closer look at one of God's creations — water. Find a pond, pool, or lake where the water is still and untroubled. Allow the placidness of the water to envelop you with its calmness. Let your negativity, pain, fear, and worry be washed away as you focus on the soothing surface of the water. Let your thoughts cease as your mind becomes smooth and peaceful like the water's surface. Hold the memory of the still water in your mind so you can return to it whenever you like.

## *Exercise 35*

## LEAVE CIVILIZATION BEHIND

### Spending Time in Nature

When I leave the city — with all its noise, crowding, and commotion — and return to nature, I find I also return to myself. Not long ago, I was alone on a sand dune while biking on Cape Cod. I was suddenly overcome by the power of silence. I was surrounded by nature, and it did not make any noise. There were no sounds from any animals or wind, and no machines, to interrupt what I felt was the loudest sound I have ever heard — silence.

I returned to myself, my thoughts, and the sounds within me. It was a scary experience, but it made me think about how indigenous cultures were forced to know themselves and be more aware of the nature of life, free from the distractions of so-called modern society.

How many of us take the time to sit quietly and listen to ourselves? For this exercise, leave the comforts of the modern world and journey to a place as far from civilization as you can. You may walk, hike, or bike, but leave your car far behind. Find a nature chapel where you can go and enjoy the silence and learn about yourself from Mother Nature's wisdom. Afterward, remember to periodically take the time to return to nature for renewal.

CHAPTER

# FIND WHAT FITS YOU BEST

*Be a self-care provider*

I prefer to be true to myself, even at the hazard
of incurring the ridicule of others, rather than to be false,
and to incur my own abhorrence.

— FREDERICK DOUGLASS

## Coaching Tip Eight

Taking good care of yourself is, for many, the hardest thing to do. Because of a lifetime of negative messages to the contrary, most people find it hard to put their needs first. When was the last time you listened to your body and responded to what it wanted emotionally and physically? Self-care should be the most important thing in your life because you are the most important person in your life. You cannot successfully nurture your soul if you don't nurture the body it inhabits.

Your level of self-esteem plays a very important

69

role in how well you take care of yourself. If you do not feel loved or acknowledged, it can lead to poor self-esteem and a lack of self-love and acceptance. Then you begin to put the needs of your job, your family, and others before your own in order to seek love and acceptance. You start to live a role and not an authentic life.

Proper self-care also means using your voice, which is exercised in chapter 4. When you are asked to do something you do not want to do, how do you respond? If you respond with a yes, then you are saying no to yourself. Many people, especially mothers, nurses, and other caregivers, have a hard time saying no to the needs of others; they are busy saving the world and nursing everyone but themselves.

On the other hand, how do you respond to those who would care for you? Do you accept help when it's offered? Or do you follow everyone else's advice except your own? For instance, if you are dealing with an illness and your doctor prescribes a treatment you do not agree with or want to experience, what should you do? You should always make your own decision. Physicians, family, and friends may want you to follow their advice, but you must have the courage to do what feels right for you. Taking care of yourself by speaking up will change the behavior of your caregivers and empower you.

Make choices that take care of you, whether it concerns a relationship, an operation, a career change, or some other event. One of my favorite quotes is, "Be what you is and not what you ain't. 'Cause if you is what you ain't, you ain't what you is." Too often I see people who awaken to life and finally take care of themselves only when they are told they have a life-threatening illness. So don't spend your life dying. Live!

# *Exercise* 36

## MAKE A NEW SCHEDULE

### Leave Time for You

For one week, your job is to pay attention to how you feel as you go from place to place and from activity to activity. Record the time spent on each activity and your feelings about it in a separate journal that you carry with you, so that at the end of the week you will have a concrete record of exactly what your week was like. Do not rely on your memory. It is easy to repress the things you don't want to deal with, so write everything down.

When the week is up, review your journal. Did you have any time during the week that you would classify as playtime? Were there any activities during which you weren't "on the clock," when you actually lost track of time? In order to create a schedule that sustains you, rather than drains you, those two elements are very necessary. Now look for places in your schedule where you could insert more quality time for yourself. What have you been wanting to do but haven't had time for? Find that time. Be sure to schedule in rest time, playtime, exercise or activities, and any classes that you've wanted to experience. Treat this as though you were an athlete creating a training schedule for the Olympics.

Finally, sit down with people close to you and review both your old schedule and your new proposed schedule. You will probably need to ask those who will be affected by any changes to help support the things you want to do. Be careful not to become defensive about your past decisions, but work with others to find ways to shift your life so it satisfies all your needs.

Remember, you do not have to change everything at once. This is a process like creating a work of art. Start re-creating your life now, and keep re-creating it over time. This is not just about making time; it is about making happiness.

## *Exercise 37*
## GIVE YOURSELF GIFTS

What Do You Want to Receive?

What do you desire? What do you think you deserve? Are these the same? What, if anything, did your parents make you feel you are worthy of, and what unworthy of? What do you pray for? Stop and think about your desires. Whether you realize it or not, you are creating your life based upon these thoughts. Take some time to yourself and make an honest appraisal of the desires that have driven your life up to now.

Is it time to rethink where you are headed and what you have been seeking for yourself? Make a new list of all the gifts you would like to receive from life — from material things to more meaningful gifts, like the gifts of time, love, and nourishment. Really focus on what it is you are seeking for yourself. What would make your life a gift? Prioritize these items. A piece of jewelry is nice, but peace of mind is of far greater value.

How many of these gifts do you already possess? Take a moment to express gratitude for them, to say thank you to yourself and to life for what you have already been given. Then consider the best ways to bestow upon yourself all the gifts that remain on your list — those that would bring you peace and a meaningful life. Believe me, you can afford what you need. The key is getting out and doing the shopping before a disaster reminds you of how short a lifetime can be.

# Exercise 38

## TAKE A BATH

Maximize Your Relaxation Time

Taking time to relax is one of the best self-care methods I know. If you have trouble resting and relaxing, remember — you *are* doing something when you rest. You are restoring and healing yourself and your life. What helps you to relax and take care of yourself?

Throughout history, baths have been a universal means of renewal and cleansing. Set aside an afternoon or evening and create a warm, healing bath for yourself, and consider incorporating a soothing bath in your weekly routine.

Make this bath more than the usual scrub. Incorporate therapeutic herbs, minerals, and bath salts, which can remove your body's impurities. Add soaps and oils with special scents and aromas to help you to relax. Candles and soft music are other ways to pamper your senses, and if you can, try an outdoor tub and add the healing sounds and scents of nature. Or, make this bath all about play — fill the tub with bubbles and give your inner child a squirt gun and some rubber ducks to play with. As every kid knows, bath time *is* play time.

## *Exercise 39*
### START A FOOD JOURNAL

Choose What's Good for You

Despite widespread concern over our physical health, most people still don't take the time to prepare healthy meals for themselves. Are you among them? Do you live off packaged snacks and fast food? If your answer is yes, I know it is not because you lack information about what makes a proper diet and why it's important. Eating the right foods keeps you healthy, extends your life, and improves your memory and emotional state.

For this exercise, you will create a food journal. Write down everything you eat for one week. Be honest and note every meal and snack, but don't judge yourself. For now, just observe. At the end of the week, review what you have written down. Where is your diet imbalanced? Is this a menu you would want your spouse or child to live on? Most likely, there will be at least a few parts of your weekly menu that need improvement.

If your diet needs lots of improvement, don't give in to the urge to criticize yourself. Love yourself, see yourself as a divine child, and then your choices will change naturally. Gently guide yourself toward making choices that both fit your lifestyle and enhance your health and well-being. As part of learning to love yourself, read and gather nutrition information, and see your doctor or a nutritionist to help you form a new food plan.

Just remember: this isn't about avoiding dying. It doesn't work. Do it to enjoy living, and receive the bonus of a longer life as a side effect. And don't forget to enjoy some chocolate ice cream now and then.

## *Exercise 40*
### INNER DIALOGUE

Tune in for Answers

In order to take better care of yourself, you have to know what your needs are. The best way to find out what nurtures your body, mind, and spirit is to ask them. Make it a habit to take the time to ask yourself, "How are you feeling?"

This is particularly important when you become overwhelmed, tired, or depressed. Stop, take a deep breath, and ask yourself, "What is the source of this discontent? Why do I feel this way? What can I do to fix it?" Sometimes the answer is a simple need for rest, while at other times the roots of your feelings stem from bigger problems. Remember not to get depressed by your feelings, but use them to guide you. Once a problem is identified, it can be resolved. When hungry, you seek nourishment, so when you are uncomfortable with your feelings, seek what will nourish you and relieve your discomfort.

One last word of advice — remember the question is about how you feel, not about how you think you should feel. Don't edit your emotions by saying, "I feel this way, but I know I shouldn't." You need to listen to your heart and not your head regarding feelings. You always know what's best for you, so take the time to ask.

# BE INSPIRED

*Supplement your diet with enthusiasm*

When you are inspired by some great purpose,
some extraordinary project, all your thoughts break
their bounds: Your mind transcends limitations, your
consciousness expands in every direction and you
find yourself in a new, great and wonderful world...
and you discover yourself to be a greater person by
far than you ever dreamed yourself to be.

— PATANJALI

## Coaching Tip Nine

Inspiration is the greatest gift because it opens your life
to many new possibilities. Each day becomes more
meaningful and your life is enhanced when your actions
are guided by what inspires you. The following exercises will help you discover what generates enthusiasm
in your life.

I encourage you to undertake both the possible and
the impossible. True inspiration overrides all fears. When
you are inspired, you enter a trance state and can accomplish things that you may never have felt capable of
doing.

Where do you find this type of inspiration? Look deep into your soul and ask yourself: "What is the purpose of being alive and living on this planet?" Your soul's response will tell you. You can also look for inspiration in various myths and parables, but it is most often found when you share your unique loving acts with others.

When your heart speaks to you about what you need to do to sustain life on this planet, listen to it, make a difference, and be an inspiration for generations to come. Be inspired by people like Gandhi, Mother Teresa, Rosa Parks, Martin Luther King, Christopher Reeve, Albert Schweitzer, Helen Keller, and many others. Now go and add your name to the list and make me proud of you. Bring your enthusiasm for life with you everywhere you go, and it will be contagious.

# *Exercise 41*

## ROLE MODEL

Someone Who Inspires You

Our culture tends to idolize people based upon superficial qualities such as physical beauty and material possessions. But are these people whose example would help us live our lives in a fulfilling way? I know from my experience how unhappy people can be when surrounded only by material goods. Even when others see them as attractive, they only see their own faults and what is lacking in their life.

The people who truly inspire us have an inner beauty. They have overcome major obstacles in their own lives and learned how to accomplish meaningful change. For this exercise, think of the people who inspire and motivate you. Whose motto can you live by? These could be famous people, family members, or others. It would be someone who, if he or she won the lottery, would ask, "Why me?" and would use the money to better the world rather than seek personal success. It would be someone who, if he or she developed a life-threatening illness, would ask, "What can I do with this?" They are people who see more than their personal circumstances.

List the qualities these people have that you would like to emulate, then hang a photo of or a symbol representing each person in a conspicuous place, so that every time you walk past, you will be reminded of what you admire about them. Strive to live your own life in a way that validates their message and makes it your own.

## *Exercise 42*

## BREATHING EXERCISES

### Inhale, Exhale

If you are interested in surviving and thriving, you must stop and take the time to breathe. Something as simple as breathing properly can make all the difference in your life; it can help you to feel invigorated and inspired.

For this exercise, practice relaxed, deep breathing. Become aware of the movement of air in and out of your nostrils and the movement of your chest and abdomen. Become aware of your body's need for oxygenation. By focusing on your body and the life-giving air you breathe into it, you will help to heal your life as a by-product.

When you are worried or disturbed, your breathing changes. You may become short of breath or hyperventilate; this can cause other symptoms and lead to physical problems because of the changes it creates in your body chemistry.

Make a point of noticing when you become worried or fearful, and in those moments, practice peaceful breathing. Become mindful of your breathing and the flow of air moving in and out of your nostrils, the movement of your chest, and inspire peace and light, and expire fear and darkness. Watch what changes occur when you do this, how the tensions throughout your body and mind are relieved. Let yourself be inspired through the deep relaxation that occurs. What inspires you will lead you to inspire. Life-enhancing activities enhance our ability to breathe in the life we are living.

# *Exercise 43*
## YOUR THEME SONG
Music for Inspiration

We all can make music, but do we find the rhythm of our lives? Listen for a moment to the sounds surrounding you right now. Is it noise or music to your ears? We are constantly surrounded by sound, but everyone experiences it differently. For some, the intensity of a city street fills them with energy, while others need the quiet of the countryside to function and find inspiration.

I use music in the operating room to help create a healing environment for patients and staff. There is a reason that certain heart rates are healthy and certain beats of music heal and relax us. Why did someone decide to have sixty seconds in a minute and not a hundred? Listen to the clock: see how the beat calms you while a more rapid beat would create tension. Films use music all the time to affect how audiences feel as they watch.

Now it is time for you to find your song, the one that speaks to you and motivates you with its words and beat. Choose a theme song for your life. Every time you hear it, you will feel excited and energized. It is your song, and it carries your message of inspiration, which leads you to embrace life.

Join me as we sing "The Impossible Dream" and live as Don Quixote did, reaching for the unreachable star.

## *Exercise 44*
## GIVE COMPLIMENTS

Say Something Nice

If you want to lift people off the ground — compliment them. Compliments are the helium that fills everyone's balloon; they elevate the person receiving them so he or she can fly over life's troubles and land safely on the other side, to be received with open arms.

When you motivate others with words of kindness, you will receive a surge of creative energy, too. I am not talking about giving false compliments to make someone feel better; I am talking about giving people the encouragement to face a challenge rather than submit to their fears. If someone you love is singing or performing in any way, your kind words can inspire the person to share his or her talents with the world. Sometimes it is the small things in life that truly help us to feel empowered. For this exercise, dedicate at least one week to giving out three genuine compliments a day, and watch how this changes the level of enthusiasm you feel toward yourself and others.

I carry pins with me that say "You Make a Difference" and give them to people I see acting in a way that is life-enhancing. Recently at the grocery store, I gave an employee a card I received as a valued customer. The card said she was special, and her smile rewarded me.

Also, remember to say thank you when compliments are sent your way. When we circulate our thanks and our compliments, the world becomes a better place.

# *Exercise 45*

## AWAKEN THE CHILD WITHIN

### Enthusiasm Is Contagious

When I am with my grandchildren, I get so involved in all their activities that my energy seems endless. Of course, by the evening I am ready for an early bedtime, but the enthusiasm and joy of my grandchildren is contagious — they bring out the child in me.

Get in touch with the playful part of you. What did you enjoy doing as a child? What interested you? What games did you love to play? Don't just visualize yourself doing those things, but get out your old games and play them again. Spend more time with children, go to playgrounds, ride a swing, go down a slide and awaken the child within you and let it communicate with the adult you are today. Ask your inner child what it wants to do. Inspiration restores you to life.

What awakens your spirit? Find a way to bring it into your life; if possible, make it the way you earn a living. If you do, you will never have to work a day in your life. At the very least find the time in your life to have the time of your life.

Without the will to live, you will go nowhere. Decide what you want and go for it with an enthusiasm that all those around you can feel. You will make your inspiration contagious, believe me, and help will appear that you never expected. The journey is what it is about — not just the destination.

# PAIN IS NECESSARY

*Life's unwanted gift*
*(you are not what you lose)*

Suffering forces us to change.
We don't like change and most of the time
we fear it and fight it. We like to remain in emotionally
familiar places even though sometimes those places are not
healthy for us. On occasion, the suffering is so great that we
have to give up. We surrender the old and begin anew.
Often it is the pain we experience that leads us, not only to
a different life, but a richer and more rewarding one.

— **DENNIS WHOLEY**

## Coaching Tip Ten

In this chapter I will ask you to see loss as a way to
strengthen your soul. This may seem strange at first, but
loss is just the inevitable result of the passage of time. As
one woman who had cancer and was about to lose a part
of her body wrote, "Do we perhaps shed things as we go
through life so that other features may be enhanced?"

I remember standing in the yard with our son, Jeff, who is a master gardener, talking about how difficult I found it pruning live plants and trees. I felt very uncomfortable cutting off a living branch. Jeff reminded me that I had no problem in the operating room cutting away parts of a person that were diseased or no longer useful. I said I could do it because it helped the person to be well, and my son said that the same was true for him when he pruned a tree or plant. His words have helped me to understand the need to give up some things in order for us to thrive and survive.

Pain and loss can be great teachers and guides. They help us to define, nourish, and protect ourselves. When we are hungry, we seek nourishment, and the experience of pain or loss leads us to do the same thing. Emotional pain becomes destructive when the loss itself becomes our only focus, rather than focusing on what we still have left. Animals have amputations and, to quote one veterinarian, "Wake up and lick their owner's faces." They are still capable of loving and feeling whole.

Fear of loss can be as painful as loss itself. We must remember that loss is part of life; it is an inevitable fact. In this light, should aging or even disability be seen as loss? Why not see them as signs of courage and sources of wisdom? I once met a young woman who was born without arms, and I learned from her not to see her as disabled but rather as incredibly enabled, for she is able to write with a pen between her toes.

You alone decide if you want to be defined by what you have lost or by who you really are. Some people cannot separate themselves from their disease and their pain; it is their way of getting attention. I prefer another choice. I define myself not by my body parts but by my spirit and attitude toward life. I try to be like the dog I know who was born with only two legs and still enjoys each day hopping around the yard.

The only time you will ever be perfect is when you leave your body. Just don't make the mistake of quitting because life hurts. Remember, you can always begin anew and find joy regardless of what your circumstances may be.

The following exercises will help you to move through your pain and losses and to find new ways to nourish yourself and those you love.

## *Exercise 46*

### TOOLS FOR HEALING

Start a Treasure Chest

As we grow and encounter life's problems and broken-ness — as we come to realize that, to quote one of our sons on a bad day, "life sucks" — most of us need help finding our way. Perhaps as we grew up we weren't given the necessary tools, or we weren't trained well in how to use them. With this exercise, you will identify and gather up the tools you need, so you'll always have them at hand.

Think about the things that you need to find your way in your life right now. What tools would help? Material, physical tools can be useful, but they are not the only answer. Even the best mechanical tools break. What emotional and spiritual tools can you have faith in and rely on? These may include a relative, a friend, prayer, or inner strength. For everyone, self-acceptance and the knowledge that you are of divine origin are essential. These spiritual tools will always be there to sustain and support you.

Now write down your list of resource tools on slips of paper. Take a small box, label it your treasure chest, and place these slips in it for safekeeping. In times of distress or trouble, open your treasure chest and take out the tools you need. Place your treasure chest where you will see it every day. Then, anytime you need help get-ting through a day, you can pull out a slip of paper to remind you of the resources you have always available.

# *Exercise 47*
## PLANT A SEED

New Life from Grief

Our family has had many pets over the years, and when they die, I always bury them in our yard. In the beginning, each time I walked by their grave sites, I would add a rock to the monument I had built. One day it occurred to me that if the pets could return and speak to me, they would tell me to bring them a flower instead. As soon as I started to do this I felt the difference in the experience. Now I was looking for something beautiful to share with their spirit and with anyone else who walked by their stone monument.

Nature does this naturally. From the dead comes new life; it nourishes and feeds what is still living. When we have a loss, we have a decision to make. What do we do with the experience? Do we remain bitter at God and life, spending our life grieving and whining, or do we start a new life and bring a flower to the world?

Reflect upon your losses and ask yourself how they can be used to create a new life. After the loss of a loved one, a great way to see new life from the grief is to plant flowers on the grave site or to create a commemorative garden for the person. For this exercise, buy a plant to honor someone who has died; tend the plant and watch it grow and signify new life. Or, donate money to plant a tree in a beloved's homeland. This will keep the cycle of birth and death continually flowing.

# *Exercise 48*

## DECIE TO GIVE

### Free Gifts

When others are suffering, how can we help? If someone has died, we cannot bring the person back, nor can we cure or fix someone else's problems. However, we can display compassion and love. We can make a gift of ourselves. When we give with no expectations, it is called love, and it is the one thing we all have to give. Our acts of love and compassion are great healers; they heal not only the one experiencing pain but our own pain as well.

For this exercise, identify someone who is suffering, and make a gift of your time and yourself to help heal the person. This could be someone you already know, like a friend or a relative, or it could be a stranger — such as someone in a senior center, nursing home, or homeless shelter. Volunteer for one day. Be willing to give freely, of yourself and your time. Learn to give and you will receive. Believe me, that is the truth. Give from your heart and watch the magic happen in two lives, that of the giver and the receiver.

*Exercise* 49

## LOOK BACK

Light from the Dark

Charcoal under pressure becomes a diamond. How many diamonds are buried in your life just waiting to be uncovered? We must learn to see life's difficulties as blessings that help us become more complete human beings. Most of us, out of fear, avoid looking at the dark moments of our lives; rather than experience pain, we choose numbness. Yet our difficulties, and how we respond to them, are what define us. For this exercise, look back at your life and identify three of your most difficult moments. Then, for each, identify something good that occurred afterward that would not have happened had the undesired event never occurred.

Life is full of redirections. The key is living in the moment and experiencing events but not letting them affect your outlook and attitude in a way that destroys your future. Keep an open mind and watch what occurs. When my father was twelve years old, his father died. It was a disaster for his family. But later in life my father called it one of the best things that ever happened to him because it taught him how to survive, to be kind and helpful to others, and to recognize what was truly valuable in life.

As you review the undesired events in your life, make sure to write down your thoughts and feelings, and to list all the unexpectedly positive outcomes. These are your diamonds. Or, to use another metaphor, these are the new plants and opportunities that grew out of the ashes and compost of your life. Teach your children, friends, and associates to keep their minds open to the future and not to become lost in events that trouble them. They will be forever grateful to you for the lesson you teach. If we choose to let them, our negative experiences can become our best teachers.

# *Exercise* 50
## EXPRESS YOUR GRIEF

Paint Your Pain

Many great artists know that grief and emotional pain can be sources of incredibly creative energy. It works the other way as well. When we engage in a creative activity, we can sometimes tap wells of deep emotion we didn't even realize existed. When you express your unresolved passion and grief through creativity, you provide yourself with a much-needed physical outlet for your pent-up emotions.

For this exercise, remember a particularly painful or difficult time, then paint your emotions. Use brushes or your fingers; choose any kind of paint and any blank surface — a canvas, white paper, or a wall. Start with any color that calls to you, splash it on, use your hands or brushes to spread it, and let the passion carry itself out through your hands onto the page. Be abstract, unless painting a scene comes naturally. You cannot do it wrong. No one will be grading your art. As you become involved in creating, you will become less aware of your body. Pay attention to your feelings; are they more, less, or different than you expected? When you are done, do not judge yourself or your creation; admire what you have created, but remember that the real learning occurs while you are creating. Remember to try this exercise any time you experience pain, loss, or deep emotions.

# FURRY FRIENDS

*The ideal role model comes with a fur coat*

Animals are such agreeable friends — they ask
no questions, they pass no criticisms.

— GEORGE ELIOT

## *Coaching Tip Eleven*

Animals are great teachers. There is no better role
model than a furry creature for demonstrating forgiveness, tolerance of others, and acceptance of criticism. In
some ways, if we all started behaving more like animals,
I think there would be a lot fewer problems in the
world. They truly teach us how to respect all shapes and
forms of life, and they confirm that the capacity to love,
feel, and reason is not limited to our species alone. Our
souls benefit when we extend our love and compassion
to all the earth's creatures, and when we in turn accept
their help and support as well.

Animals can play many roles in your life, from friend to companion to protector. They bring you joy and laughter. Caring for an animal — whether a dog, cat, hamster, bird, or goldfish — will help you to know yourself better and live a healthier life. In an Australian study, those who suffered a heart attack and went home to a house containing a dog had a death rate of less than 6 percent the following year; those who had no dog at home had a death rate closer to 30 percent. Do you want to save on medical expenses? Get a dog!

I always teach people that when in doubt — when you aren't sure what the right thing to do is — to remember WWLD. In other words, what would Lassie do? Lassie was always kind, loyal, protective, and motivated by love. Also, when dealing with others, I try to follow a veterinarian's expert advice for dog training: Use rewards rather than punishment; always show love, trust, and respect; and make a commitment to consistency.

Our children learned to have a reverence for life because our land and home were filled with animals of all species. The one hundred animals we cared for were less trouble than our five children. The pets never had an unkind word to say, even when I accidentally locked them outside.

The following exercises will help you to make some new furry friends.

## *Exercise 51*

### PICK A FAVORITE

Animal Qualities

The animal kingdom contains many diverse species, each with a distinct personality and unique abilities. Though we may all have similar structures and colors on the inside, we are very different on the outside. I believe that is for recognition and to enhance our unique abilities, authenticity, and individuality.

Do you already have a favorite animal? If not, think of one now. What animal do you relate to and admire because of its special qualities and personality? Write down a list of characteristics and personality traits that attract you to this specific creature. Now read the list to people who know you well and ask them, who do they think it describes? Right, it's you.

You can think of this animal as your totem or special teacher, emulate it in your life, and call on it for guidance as needed. As time goes on and you change, so may your totem animal take different forms.

## *Exercise 52*

# HELP AN ANIMAL IN NEED

### A Helping Hand

The benefits of helping others extend to the animal kingdom as well. It is a satisfying and rewarding experience to lend a hand, whether it is at an animal shelter, zoo, rally, or in your front yard by turning it into a certified wildlife sanctuary.

For this exercise, choose one way to help animals in need. One of the best and easiest ways is to go to your local animal shelter and volunteer for a day. Ask if you can help by walking the dogs, petting or feeding the cats, or socializing the animals. If you can, make this a regular event. But be careful: even if you don't intend to adopt an animal, you may find one of them adopts you. If permanently adopting an animal isn't feasible, you and the animals will still benefit from your time with them at the shelter.

Other options might include volunteering to pet sit for one of your neighbors. You could act as a temporary foster home for newborn puppies and kittens. There are many animal organizations, such as guide dogs for the blind, that could use volunteers or support through your donations. Think about what skills and talents you have to offer. Perhaps you can write a newsletter for an animal organization, help plan a fund-raiser, rescue or transport abused animals to new homes, or help build a shelter. You know your skills, so let your heart lead the way.

## *Exercise 53*
## ANIMAL STORIES

Read a Good Book

There are many wonderful books describing what animals can teach us and how they help to humanize us. A great one to start with is *Animals as Teachers and Healers*, which was written by my friend Susan Chernak McElroy. As you read the animal stories in her book, many lessons will surface that you can incorporate into your life.

When I was growing up I used to read all the Lassie stories, and I still love them. Reading stories about animals and their experiences and behavior is a wonderful way to teach your children about values and kindness as well. There are books on animal communication that can teach you how to communicate and live in harmony with your pet. I know from experience that it really works. Animals are incredibly intuitive, and I am sure you have all heard stories of how they rescue drowning children or run for help when someone is injured and can't move.

Susan McElroy's animal story is as amazing as any. Susan was diagnosed with cancer and told she had a year to live. She lived alone, and one day she let a stray cat into her house for company. She named the cat Flora and took her to a vet to be sure she was healthy. The vet examined Flora and told Susan that Flora had feline leukemia and a year to live. Susan came home totally depressed, but she noticed her cat wasn't. So she thought, maybe Flora knows something I don't. Susan started acting like Flora, taking naps, asking for what she needed, and living her dreams, and as a result, they are both still alive over fourteen years later.

Find a book about animals that calls to you and allow a new furry friend to enter your life from the pages.

# *Exercise 54*
## ADOPT A FRIEND

Open Your Home and Your Heart

The United States has an abundance of homeless dogs and cats. Animal shelters are full of loving critters with so much to give, who are just looking for a new owner to take them home. This exercise requires more of a commitment than most of the others in this book. It asks you to adopt a pet. If you already have a pet and can't take another, or if keeping a pet isn't feasible for you, at least consider following the instructions in exercise 52.

Look over your living quarters and think about what kind of pet would be a good match. I frequently talk about our cats and dogs, but we have had snakes, fish, chameleons, goats, birds, and many other species in our home. Consider your entire lifestyle when deciding what kind of animal to adopt. If you travel frequently, a dog that needs lots of personal attention may not be a good fit; consider fish or a reptile instead. Whatever you choose, make space for it and get the supplies you need to create a healthy habitat.

When you are ready, go to the local pet store or animal shelter. Another alternative is to take a vacation with your family and visit one, such as Best Friends' Animal Sanctuary in Utah, which is doing wonderful things rescuing all kinds of animals. You may have a certain animal in mind, but let your heart pick the new friend to bring home when you get to the shelter. Or do what I do and let the new friend pick you. When I walk into a shelter, I wait to see who runs over to embrace me, then we go home together and ask my wife, Bobbie, to let us both in.

## *Exercise* 55
### TIME TO PLAY
Roll and Fetch

Pets make great playmates and will help to bring out the child in you. When we interact with adults, we are often concerned with what they will think of our behavior. However, with a dog, you can get down on the floor and roll around and play. Not only is this good for the heart and the blood pressure, but it is good for your peace of mind. Many studies verify the benefits of interacting with pets, no matter what type they are. Our dogs love to have tummy rubs, and at times they will walk into the center of a support group I am working with and roll over. I always point out to the group that dogs are therapists, too, and they are teaching us to ask for what we need, whether it's a tummy rub, a hug, or a special snack.

Take your pets with you when you go places. Going for walks with your dog will increase your health and longevity. We have a cat, named Miracle, who thinks she is a dog and will walk on a leash and keep me company wherever I go. Miracle has no fear, and once I even entered her in a dog show, where she sat among dozens of dogs who found her quite interesting.

So, for this exercise, simply play with your pet, each and every day. Let your pet teach you how to loosen your inhibitions and restore your joy in living.

Animals live in the moment and can help us to do the same, to let go of our fears and our worries about tomorrow. Our pets know that worrying does not solve anything, while a tummy rub or nap can do a great deal.

# DREAMS, DRAWINGS, AND SYMBOLS

*The blank canvas can become
a work of art*

Imagination is the outreaching of mind...the
bombardment of the conscious mind with ideas,
impulses, images and every sort of psychic phenomena
welling up from the preconscious. It is the capacity
to dream dreams and see visions.

— ROLLO MAY

## Coaching Tip Twelve

Why didn't God create a common language we could all
speak so that communicating would be easier? Actually,
there is a universal language, the language of symbols,
that speaks to us all. And we are all capable of accessing
this language through our dreams and imaginations.

I believe we sleep in order to allow the part of our
mind that connects us to the Greater Consciousness to
have a chance to express itself. Many solutions to problems and creative ideas come through dreams. By working with our dreams, we can learn an amazing amount
about the inner landscape of our psyches and souls.

Symbols are both discovered and invented. The meanings associated with them come from a deep place within us that connects to the whole of creation. Anyone can draw symbols, and anyone can understand them. I can travel anywhere on this planet with a box of crayons and interpret drawings by people whose spoken language I cannot understand. When I see a circle, or a triangle, it can represent different aspects of the personality. When I see a tree, it may be symbolic of an entire life.

Take the time to pay attention to your dreams, draw when you are in conflict, and let the symbols that emerge lead you. Thinking alone cannot tap the mysteries of the mind. The following exercises will provide you with several methods to begin to use dreams, drawings, and symbols to create a more meaningful life.

# Exercise 56
## DREAM JOURNAL
### Understand Your Dreams

When you work with your dreams, you will find yourself becoming more aware in your waking life. Many people record their dreams and work to become conscious in their dreams as a mode of self-therapy. Others use dreams to answer specific questions in their lives.

For at least one week, keep a dream journal, though I highly recommend writing in a dream journal as an ongoing practice. Before you go to sleep at night, ask a question for your unconscious to respond to; you could write that question on a slip of paper and place it under your pillow. Keep your journal and a pencil at your bedside, and when you wake in the morning, or anytime you wake up, write down whatever dream or dreams you remember.

Everything in the dream is a part of you. Write down all the images and experiences in as much detail as you can remember. Act as though you are explaining your dream to an extraterrestrial and describe everything.

Dream language is symbolic. The meaning of some symbols may be immediately obvious, while others are more elusive. The longer you pay attention to your dreams, the better you will be able to interpret them. If a dream keeps repeating itself, it is because you are not responding to what it is telling you or asking of you. Pay close attention to repetitive dreams for deeper messages about your life, and in general be sure to note any recurring themes.

## *Exercise 57*
### MEANINGFUL SYMBOLS
Creating a Mandala for Personal Reflection

The use of symbols can be a very effective tool for gaining insight. The word *mandala* is Sanskrit for "circle." The mandala is an ancient Indian symbol representing wholeness, and it can reveal much about the unconscious. In Tibetan Buddhism it is used as a means of contemplation. For this exercise, you will create your own personal mandala that represents the different aspects of yourself.

On a sheet of paper, draw a large circle. The circle can be divided into quarters, with each section representing a different aspect of your life. It can also be split across the middle, with the top representing your soul and spirit, and the bottom representing your body and earthly possessions. Decide how you would like to divide your circle and what each section will represent, and consider what symbols, colors, and designs to include. Be creative.

Each object you draw should have significance to you and represent your vision. Let intuition guide you as much as possible. When you think of your body, what colors, patterns, deities, animals, and symbols come to mind? Don't second-guess your choices, and it's okay to practice with several designs before deciding on a final one.

When you are finished creating this personal symbol, hang it somewhere where you can meditate on the image and let it speak to you.

# Exercise 58

## GET YOUR OWN CRAYONS

What Does Creative Vision Say about You?

All adults should have their own large box of crayons. They are a wonderful tool for self-expression. For this exercise, pick up a box with a full spectrum of colors and a good-size tablet of drawing paper. Then do the following:

### Step One:

Draw a picture of an outdoor scene, and include a tree in it. Do not read step two until you have completed the drawing.

### Step Two:

Interpret your drawing. Now notice how empty or full the picture is. What colors did you choose? This drawing represents your life and the tree represents you. Knowing that, what does your drawing say about how you feel about your environment and yourself? Are you blooming or waning? How important are you in the scheme of things?

## *Exercise* 59
### FINDING PENNIES
Look for Symbols

As you walk along what you believe to be your divine path through life, pay attention to the messages you receive during your everyday activities to verify that you are on the right track. In my own life I look for pennies as a symbol that I am moving in the right direction and in the right place. Every time I find a penny, it reaffirms that I am on the correct course. I use it as a message confirming the direction of my life.

Once I have found a penny, my chosen symbol, I keep it in my pocket so I can always reach in when I need reassurance. It is a reminder that I can find meaning in the most unthinkable places. In fact, I have a jar at my house filled with pennies that I use to spread around for other people to find, too!

For one week, look for symbols along your life path and let them guide you in the right direction.

# *Exercise* 60

## HEALING SYMBOLS

### Create a Personal Altar

Throughout history, people have used altars to create a tangible point of focus for prayer, meditation, and beauty. The creation and use of an altar can enhance your sense of well-being and provide many benefits. It offers a place to focus your energy, ask for divine guidance, and show your gratitude.

You can create a personal altar in your home or office. First decide what you want your altar to look like and what it will be made out of. You want it to bring a feeling of peace to you when you approach it, so select materials such as silk, flowers, or colorful stones — something that you find tranquil.

Next decide the purpose you are creating your altar for. What are you seeking? You can design altars to attract material desires as well as to meet soulful and spiritual needs. Select objects that have significance for you. You might choose statues of symbolic or religious figures such as Wan Yin, the Buddhist goddess of compassion, or other mythic figures and goddesses. Nothing that has meaning to you is inappropriate. Other options might be feathers, candles, bells, flowers, candy hearts, shells, cards, belongings and gifts from loved ones, or photographs.

After your altar is completed, focus on your intention and the feeling you receive from your creation.

Spend time in front of the altar in prayer or meditation and allow answers and direction to come from the divine. Then give thanks and return to the world and utilize what you have received.

# MOTIVATION

*Get up and get going*

Motivation is not a matter of will-power,
it is a matter of want-power.

— **PAUL KARASIK**

## Coaching Tip Thirteen

Some days it is just plain difficult to find the motivation
to get up and do anything. Finding out what motivates
you is very important in order to fully participate in
life. Without motivation many opportunities will pass
you by.

What does it take to get you motivated? Do you need
to feel an inner passion first? Does the thought of helping
others drive you? Or is it hard for you to get motivated
unless you are threatened by some bad consequence? All
three are probably true at some time, and just as hunger
drives us to eat, sometimes pain and depression motivate

us to nourish ourselves, ultimately becoming resources for our own survival.

Fear can be a great motivator, too, though it can also paralyze you if you let it. I remember a story that the Reverend Norman Vincent Peale, who wrote *The Power of Positive Thinking*, told several years ago. A man walked home from work every night through a cemetery in order to shorten his journey considerably. One night, as he was walking through the cemetery, he fell into a freshly dug grave. Try as he might, he couldn't climb out because the sides kept crumbling. He finally gave up, and when no one responded to his shouts for help, he made himself comfortable and prepared to spend the night in the grave. About an hour later he was awakened when another man fell into the grave. The other fellow had no idea there was someone else in the grave, and he started to try and climb out. The first man, trying to be helpful, said, "It's no use. You will never climb out of this grave." Upon hearing those words, the second man shot up the side of the grave and out the top like a shell out of a cannon.

So whatever it takes for you to get up and get going, do it! The following exercises will help you to discover what motivates you.

# Exercise *61*

## CORE MOTIVATIONS

Reward Systems

Is it easier for you to get motivated to accomplish a task if there is a reward waiting for you at the end? Rewards can be very helpful motivators, though if seeking a reward becomes your main motivation in all circumstances, then your self-interest will get in the way of core motivations like compassion and generosity. When more selfless emotions guide you, you will reward yourself and the people your actions touch far beyond your expectations.

However, setting up a small reward system to help motivate yourself can be positive and useful. For this exercise, identify one or two tasks that you've found it difficult to accomplish — things that you perhaps do not feel passionate about but which you still need to do — and set up a reward system. Divide the task into pieces, and give yourself something to look forward to after you complete each piece. Rewards might include taking yourself to the movies or going out for a special dinner.

When you finish the task, notice how well the rewards worked. Did they make a difference? What other, nonmaterial rewards could you replace them with? Dig deep and find out what your core motivations are. What does your choice of rewards say about them?

# Exercise 62

## TURN THE KEY

### What Car Do You Drive?

When you get into your car, you have to turn the ignition key to get it started. Is something keeping you from turning your key, stepping on the accelerator, and getting your life moving? Do you feel stuck in reverse or unable to shift out of low gear because you are afraid to move forward and take a risk?

Maybe the problem is the type of car you drive. For this exercise, imagine yourself as a vehicle — what would you be? A bus or a sports car? A mobile home or a tow truck? Sometimes we develop an image of ourselves, or slip into roles, that are unsatisfying, and so we lose our motivation. If that's true for you, metaphorically test-drive a new car this week. If you've been a tow truck — and spend all your time rescuing everyone else — and you long to slip into a sports car, do it! Don't start careening recklessly through life, but don't be afraid to change your self-image and step on the gas a little.

There is nothing wrong with being a tow truck if it gives your life meaning. But stop and ask yourself if you are in the right vehicle and heading in the right direction. I know of a woman who demolished her new car. It had cruise control, so she pushed the button and then started to do her hair. She explained to the police she thought the cruise control took care of everything. This woman didn't understand her vehicle — so think about what would be the right vehicle to get you to your destination.

# *Exercise* 63

## SPRING CLEANING

Make Room for the New

As we travel through life, we collect a great deal of real and metaphorical baggage, and our inspirations and motivations can get buried underneath this pile of accumulated stuff. Part of the way we can care for ourselves is to periodically release all the negativity of the past and make room for positive new growth. Your task for this exercise is to start your renewal now by physically and emotionally cleaning out all your clutter and excess belongings. Whatever the season, it's time for a spring cleaning.

Start with the obvious physical items in your closets, drawers, and kitchen cabinets. Get rid of everything you no longer use; one way to determine if something is still useful is to ask yourself if you've used it within the past year. If you haven't, dump it. Donate useable items to your favorite charity. For sentimental items, dispose of them in a little ceremony, pledging to keep the memories even as you get rid of the physical reminder. Then reorganize everything you have retained.

As you purge your belongings, however, don't be too ruthless. Sometimes old items can be dusted off and put to good, new uses; others may be too significant to part with. You can create a new beginning and get rid of old baggage without entirely starting over.

When you are done, you will have room to give birth to a new life. Without clear space to grow in, you cannot come out into the light of day.

# Exercise 64

## DAILY MOTIVATION

### Read Each Day

There are many books, websites, and newsletters that offer daily doses of inspiration. These provide little reminders that keep us on the right path, and for this exercise, find at least one that works for you and use it. Ask your friends or at your local bookstore for some good book referrals. Look for a book with entries for every day of the year. Keep one by your bedside, one at the breakfast table, and one at work. Fold the corners of important pages down and underline key passages so you can focus on certain messages on days you really feel the need for inspiration and motivation. One message that sits before me on my desk says, "Peace comes when you relinquish desires, not from achieving them."

You can keep a motivational CD in the car to listen to as you drive, and you can put your computer on the task as well. To see what's available online, type the words "motivational sites" into a search engine like www.google.com. Two websites that will send you daily inspirational messages are www.thedailymotivator.com and www.strategiesforliving.com.

Whatever method you use, work to keep yourself focused and your mind at peace every day.

# *Exercise* 65

## SMALL EFFORTS

One Step at a Time

Sometimes when you find your motivation and energy are severely lacking, it may be best to give yourself permission to put a task aside and rest. When you do this, give yourself a free pass from guilt and blame. For this exercise, identify a long-term project that for one reason or another you haven't been able to complete, and for the moment, let it go.

Then, when your energy and motivation return, start slowly. Don't try to make up for lost time, but keep going steadily until you get tired. A gentle pace will allow you to remain motivated longer and help you complete your task without burning out. At times, starting with small efforts can help you build momentum until a project becomes so interesting and satisfying you start attacking it eagerly. It's then that you will begin to venture beyond your normal boundaries — to think outside the box, as the saying goes — and things will get really exciting.

Break the job down into small steps. Every journey begins with one step, and if you keep moving, you will get to the finish line. When I run a marathon, I take it one step at a time and don't think about how far I have to go. I just focus on moving forward, and eventually I make it to the finish line. Once I heard a woman spectator say, "You are all winners." I will never forget her gift. So get moving, and you will find that not every mile of a marathon is hard; some are downhill and easy.

# BE AN ACTIVIST

*Get involved — do it now*

Throughout your life, there is a voice only you can hear. A voice which mythologists label "the call." A call to the value of your life. The choice of risk and individual bliss over the known and secure. You may choose not to hear your spirit. You may prefer to build a life within the compound, to avoid risk. It is possible to find happiness within a familiar box, a life of comfort and control. Or, you may choose to be open to new experiences, to leave the limits of your conditioning, to hear the call. Then you must act. If you never hear it, perhaps nothing is lost. If you hear it and ignore it, your life is lost.

— JENNIFER JAMES

## Coaching Tip Fourteen

It is a proven fact: when we help others, we help ourselves. One of the best workouts for your soul, and a surefire way to add greater meaning in your life, is to become involved in a good cause or a charitable organization. The first step is to get up and get yourself moving. When you move, it literally changes your body chemistry. Studies have shown that antidepressant-type chemicals are created in your body when you walk and exercise. In addition, volunteers live longer, healthier lives. I remember when the AIDS epidemic started that those who were HIV-positive and who volunteered to help others stayed healthier longer.

When you become an activist or a volunteer, you are working to change more than your personal circumstances, and you will find yourself filled with energy. The rewards for your efforts extend from yourself and those you love to the entire world.

So get moving and get involved. What you do isn't the issue, as long as you are doing something. You can camp in the top of a redwood to save the trees, or volunteer to help those in need in your town or on the other side of the world — do whatever has meaning for you. Quantum physicists tell us desire and intention can change the world.

The following exercises will help guide your journey to find your heart's calling and motivate you to become more involved.

## *Exercise* 66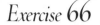

## VOLUNTEER

Get Involved

Volunteering is very important for creating a meaningful life. It helps define what you are here to accomplish by actively doing it. For this exercise, choose one way to volunteer in your community, and make it more than a one-shot deal. Think about what the right form of service is for you. What skills do you have? What do you enjoy doing? Who would you like to serve? Has a friend or relative been challenged by an illness or disability that you'd like to help combat? Have you? Is there a political issue that makes you burn? Whatever you decide, the key is simple: find a way to serve living things, whether people, animals, or nature.

Activities that I personally feel most passionate about and that I have used to help the community around me include volunteering at animal shelters, at schools, and at nursing homes and participating in scouts and Big Brothers' and Sisters' programs. Other ways I try to help are by collecting roadside recyclables, by shoveling snow or mowing the lawn for senior neighbors, by carrying and packing bundles at the supermarket checkout counter, by contributing to charities such as Habitat for Humanity, and by putting up signs and reflectors on town roads to make them safer. So get up, get moving, and help out!

## Exercise 67

## START A CLUB

### Share Interests and Help Out

Another constructive way to help your community is to start a club with other people who have similar interests and hobbies. Consider this exercise an alternative volunteer option for exercise 66. When you have a common desire or interest, things get done. Are you concerned about neighborhood parks or schools? Others are, too, and you could be the force that organizes them. Do you have a hobby like bird-watching? You could gather other local bird-watchers with a goal to create a bird sanctuary or to help set up bird feeders in the wild. Some of the most passionate clubs I know are organized to slow down development in communities and preserve natural open areas.

You could start with a neighborhood party so that people get to know one another and then set up a community watch program. By taking responsibility for your community, even in a small way, you increase your social network and create a warmer atmosphere. Working to realize the community's shared values keeps you active and improves the lives of everyone.

## *Exercise 68*

### LIVE IN SOMEONE ELSE'S SHOES

Compassion and Caring

To truly be an activist, you need to understand what others are feeling and sincerely care about them and their plight. What you do not experience can be difficult to fully understand. Tourists and natives live a very different experience. I know as a doctor that I did not truly understand my patients' experience until I was a patient. When you step outside of your own experiences, you broaden your perspective and begin to take on a humanistic approach to life.

For this exercise, choose someone whose life is nearly the opposite of yours and visualize yourself in that person's place; become aware of how you feel and how the person might feel and why. What difficulties does this person face that you don't? How would you handle them if you did? When you acknowledge those with more troubles than you and reach out to help them, it provides your life with meaning. By becoming unselfish in thought and deed, you take the emphasis off your own troubles, and when you do this, you will be surprised by how much better you feel about your life.

The next time you see or meet someone who is down on their luck, think of what that must feel like and how the person might have gotten there. Be kind. If you offer nothing more than your time and thoughtfulness, you will make a difference.

# *Exercise* 69

## REMEMBER YOUR CORE BELIEFS

### What Do You Stand For?

What is it you really believe in? Who or what is your life's Lord? For this exercise, make a list of your true beliefs. When you are done, consider in what ways each one affects your life and the decisions you make. Are you realizing these core beliefs in all your actions?

If not, then what beliefs are actually guiding you? Make a second list of these "unhealthy" beliefs, the ones that lead you to make negative choices. Of course, we don't normally call our negative impulses "beliefs," but they function in the same way. And they can keep us from matching our actions with our desires.

Now consider all the ways that your negative actions would change if they were driven by your core beliefs. Ideally, how would you bring beauty and hope into the world in a way that represents the person you want to be? Make a final list of the things you can do that you haven't done yet to realize your core beliefs in your life and the world. Keep this list where you can refer to it often, and do this exercise again whenever you feel like your life does not exemplify what you believe.

If you have a problem coming up with these beliefs, refer back to some of the great teachers, such as Buddha, or the teachings found in the Bible. Read about the sages of the past, their struggles, and the efforts they made to teach others how to avoid life's painful lessons.

Be willing to stand up for what you believe in, tell others, write about it, and lobby for the things you want changed.

## *Exercise 70*

# BE A SELF-ACTIVIST

### Fight for Your Rights

The world is overwhelmed by oppression: oppression of ideas, feelings, and people. In general, we tend to focus on the differences in others rather than on the many similarities we share. We become our own oppressors. Resist this tendency and speak out for what you believe in. Speak out for those who cannot speak for themselves. By helping them you are helping yourself and making the world a more liberated and humane place to live. Express your feelings, thoughts, and words. Your views are important. You are a member of this species, and there are many things you can do and say to change things for the better.

Find the courage to fight for your beliefs, whether it is speaking out on the political candidate you plan to vote for or rallying against the shopping mall they are planning to build around the corner. Your voice deserves to be heard. What you want and need matters. Forget the inhibiting messages of your past and embrace your ability to communicate and enlighten the world around you.

CHAPTER

# SPIRITUAL CALISTHENICS

*Exercise from within*

That is happiness; to be dissolved
into something completely great.

— **WILLA CATHER**

## Coaching Tip Fifteen

There is an extremely beneficial type of exercise that can be done anywhere and anytime. It does require a certain amount of focus and discipline, but it offers benefits that will enhance your entire life. The type of exercise I am talking about is spiritual calisthenics.

I said spiritual, not religious, because sometimes they do not mean the same thing. I think many of the prophets and sages of the past, such as Jesus and Buddha, set a good example of how we can live spiritually while not being overly focused on rituals and theology. I think organized religions are important, and I have learned much from them about how to live. But the spiritual calisthenics in this chapter are nondenominational exercises that anyone can practice to help live a better life. If you understand the history and meaning behind a religion's rituals, and practice them for those reasons, they can be healing. But when rituals are practiced without understanding, they become meaningless and troublesome.

There are many types of simple spiritual exercises that can enhance your life; these include daily periods of prayer and meditation to quiet your intellect and find your spiritual connection, several types of yoga, reading spiritual texts, and listening to lectures by wise men and women who can guide and inspire you. Spiritual practice will sustain you while bringing you peace and wisdom. Nor do you need to seek alone. Be a student and use the teachings of those you admire to help you find your spiritual path. The wisdom of the sages and ages will save you from much suffering.

# *Exercise 71*

## FOLLOW THE SUN

### Sunrise, Sunset

There is a natural cycle and rhythm to each day. The sun comes up and the sun sets. Most people's lives are so busy that they lose the connection with this natural cycle. Life is a cycle, too: a circle of birth and death marked in between by spiritual events and rituals. We are all connected, and this connection is what keeps us alive.

Set aside a day away from work and obligations to observe a full day's cycle. Go somewhere where you will have an unobstructed view of the sky; the seashore or a mountaintop are ideal. Wake up before the sun rises and watch the first rays of light appear, then follow the sun as it progresses over the horizon and the day comes to life. Throughout the day, take note of how plants, animals, and people respond to the sun's phases, from sunrise to sunset. Become aware of the natural rhythm of a day. In the evening, make sure to watch the sunset from the same place you watched the sunrise, and spend some portion of the evening observing the quieter rhythms of the night.

Discard your troubles with the new day and accept the circle of life. As you go through your days, do not accumulate all the troubles of the past. Abandon them in the dark of night, and awaken refreshed with the light of day.

## *Exercise 72*

## MEDITATE

### Go Inside

Meditation has been used through the years by many as a means to relax and connect with the divine. Modern-day life is full of distractions, and meditation is a method of putting those distractions aside. How often do you take the time to sit and listen to yourself or just have a quiet moment?

When I suggest to people that they try meditation, I find a large number of them end up feeling guilty if they don't do it exactly and as often as I suggest. However, meditation works best when it is not approached too formally. If you spend moments simply enjoying your day, that is a form of meditation as well.

The point of meditation is to find inner peace and a higher level of awareness. Meditation increases your mindfulness and makes you aware of the nature of life. It is a type of healing that comes from within, from the conscious wisdom of your heart and mind. There are many types of meditation, and for this exercise you should incorporate one style into your daily routine. The simplest meditation is just sitting quietly, eyes closed, and listening to what is going on inside you. However, you can easily find books and CDs to help guide you in finding other forms and styles of meditation; some incorporate chanting or spoken words as well as physical movements or exercises. Do not let specific

formats trouble you. Remember, you do not have to follow a rigid format to accomplish a healing meditation.

You can meditate while walking, sitting, listening
to music, or reading words of wisdom, and the end
result can be the same. A good meditation always leads
you to a higher state of consciousness and a new level of
awareness.

## *Exercise* 73
## COMMUNICATE WITH THE DIVINE
### Send Blessings

Every day I pray for those I love and care about, as well as for those who make my life difficult. I even pray for people I don't know if they are affecting my life. I pray for myself as well, but frankly I am more concerned with the lives of my loved ones than I am with my own, so I devote more time to them.

Scientific research has shown that blessing people in prayer is more effective than making specific requests. So what I do, and suggest you do, is send blessings and bathe your loved ones in a healing light so that their needs will be taken care of.

Why do I also pray for people who are driving me crazy? Because it frees me from their grasp and helps me to see them in a different light. I also begin to understand them better, and through that understanding I find forgiveness for them and myself.

For this exercise, incorporate prayer into your daily life. Find a method of prayer that works for you. Communicate with the divine and pray for yourself, those you love, those you don't, and to help the world become a more peaceful and love-filled place.

# *Exercise* 74
## GUIDANCE SYSTEMS

Spiritual Assistance

I often mention in my lectures Jung's statement that the future is unconsciously prepared long in advance and, therefore, can be guessed by clairvoyants. However, if you want to save money, you can learn about your future at no significant cost. I personally am fascinated by, and use, the I Ching and Angel cards or Medicine cards. I have also tried runes, tarot cards, and a Ouija board.

Ancient people used these tools of divination to aide in their spiritual growth partly because they were more open-minded to the nature of life and wisdom; they were not obsessed with technology, as we often are. As they knew, there are many ways to communicate with the conscious and unconscious mind.

For this exercise, expand your mind and try some of these spiritual divination systems. You may be amazed by the guidance they make available to you that your intellect has shut out. I have witnessed many fascinating experiences at various meetings using drums, gongs and bells, crystal balls, pendulums, astrology, and past-life regression. If it is therapeutic, I am willing to experience it. So let your angel speak to you. Just don't tell your therapist — unless he or she is open-minded and holistic, too.

## *Exercise 75*
## WHAT IS YOUR ROLE?

### Our Significance

Sometimes I introduce myself as an outside consultant to the Board of Directors of Heaven. We all have many roles in our life, such as parent, child, wage earner, teacher, lover, and more. Yet we all have a greater role as well; we are all part of the spiritual whole. We are no less significant than any part of the universe. We are made of the divine stuff from which everything comes — from the great undifferentiated, intelligent, loving energy. Know you are part of the divine family, and there is work for you to do.

For the next ten days, think of yourself as God's (or Spirit's) right hand. Each day remember this as you make your decisions on what to do and what to say. You have a special role; what you do matters. Ask yourself, How can I help? How can I make a difference? Remember who you truly are and act accordingly.

CHAPTER

# 16

# DO WHAT YOU FEAR

*Embrace fear and watch it fall asleep in your arms*

I must not fear. Fear is the mind-killer.
Fear is the little-death that brings total obliteration.
I will face my fear. I will permit it to pass over me and
through me. And when it has gone past I will turn the
inner eye to see its path. Where the fear has gone there
will be nothing. Only I will remain.

— FRANK HERBERT

## Coaching Tip Sixteen

When you find your life limited by fear, look closely at
exactly what you are afraid of. Until you define and face
your fears, there can be no resolution. Whenever someone talks to me about his or her fears, I ask the person to
define and describe them in detail so we are not dealing
with some vague concept. The most common fears have
to do with dying, losing a job, or getting a divorce, but I
have to know what these mean to each individual.
When we define our fears, we realize we are not power-
less and can make changes.

Using visualization will help you to overcome your
fears. Start by visualizing exactly what you fear and

then visualize a successful outcome. Fear happens when you visualize an unsuccessful outcome, whether it concerns a job application or a cancer diagnosis. You can reprogram yourself and improve your life. I teach people to see their fear as a crying infant. Pick it up and embrace it and then watch what happens to the infant and your fears. Learning to embrace fear will restore you to life.

There are people who fear going outside, and they live as recluses. Why are they afraid? Why not go out and live and stop worrying about what could happen, or what others think? I know people who were cured of agoraphobia when they developed a life-threatening illness. That is, when they really had something to worry about, they dropped the small stuff. But it is all small stuff. We have to realize that everything we fear others have already lived through and survived, and we all are of the same species.

The exercises provided in this chapter offer tools to help you define, embrace, and overcome your fears.

# *Exercise* 76
## WHAT ARE YOU AFRAID OF?

Experience Fear and Embrace It

Face and embrace what you fear and it will become smaller. When you confront fear, the monster that seems to be threatening you will become a little lizard. But if you keep running, the monster will never cease chasing you. Don't wait for a life-threatening illness to give yourself permission to take a chance and face your fears.

For this exercise, think of something you have always feared doing and do it. This could be something you've always wanted to do but were afraid to fail at — such as a sport like skiing or an activity like singing in public — or it could be something that directly addresses a phobia. If you are afraid of heights, then skydive, ride a roller coaster, or fly in a small plane. If you are agoraphobic, just going out in public might be a heroic act.

Once you've decided what it is you will do, first take the time to visualize yourself doing the event successfully and fearlessly. See yourself taking part in this activity comfortably. Some relaxing music in the background can help. As you see things occurring, experience the feelings that come to your awareness. At the end of the visualization, see yourself smiling and feeling successful.

Then put your plans in motion. Follow through and do it. Take a chance. Become a kid again, free of the inhibitions and fears imposed by adults. You might just enjoy it!

## *Exercise 77*

# PUT YOUR FEARS AWAY

### Storage Box

Many of us become preoccupied with our fears and worries. They become like familiar companions and occupy our thoughts day after day. There is a lot to be said for the saying "Out of sight, out of mind." While we don't want to become unconscious of our fears and the way they affect us, for this exercise we will create a new home for them.

Pick out a special box, something small and secure, and then use it to create a sanctuary for your fears and worries. Every time you notice fear surfacing, write down what it is you are afraid of and the event that created the feeling and challenged your peace of mind. Keep these notes sealed in your storage box, and visualize that once they are in the box, they are being turned over to divine guardians for safekeeping.

Periodically go through the box and review your notes. Your fears will eventually dissolve, and when they do, discard the notes related to them. Eventually, the contents of the storage box will all end up at the dump, buried under the landfill, and you will no longer have to see or feel them ever again.

## *Exercise 78*

### SEEK TO RESOLVE

Practical Solutions

Most of our fears have their roots in our childhoods. Before we are fully formed, we receive messages from and pick up the problems of others: our parents, teachers, and other authority figures. Some of us were taught to expect the worst and were provided with no resources to overcome our fears. As adults, our problems stem not so much from the way the world treats us as from the way we first learned to approach it.

This exercise is designed to help you move through your fears. Get a sheet of lined paper and make two columns. In the column on the left, make a list of your fears, one at a time. Carefully express and define exactly what it is you are afraid of. In the column on the right, write the steps that need to be taken in order to resolve the problems that your fears create. Some solutions may be personal and others practical. Where and how can you change yourself and your life by such things as reaching out to others and altering your beliefs and behavior?

Now assign a number to each of your fears based upon how significant they are in your life. When you are done, select one to work on and begin today. Sometimes it is easier to start with lesser fears to build your confidence and ability to change. Until then, act as if you are the person you want to be, and fake it 'til you make it.

## *Exercise 79*
### FACE IT
#### You Can Handle It

The next time you find your mind obsessing on a particular fear, try this effective exercise. I have used it for years, and it always resolves my worries.

Say I have a very important lecture to give in another city. On the way to the airport I am caught in a horrible traffic jam, and I am afraid I will miss my plane. The situation seems hopeless, and I become agitated, worried, fearful, and seeking solutions that don't exist. Rather than tell myself not to worry, I consider how I would respond to each worry, taking my fears to their worst-case scenario. What will I do if I miss the plane? What if there are no more flights? What if I never get out of traffic? How long can I last without food, sanitary facilities, and no heat? Who will find my emaciated body weeks from now? By the time the drama has ended, I am laughing and a lot more relaxed. I know the world won't end if I miss the plane, and I've thought through a few ways I'll handle missing the plane if I do. Who knows, maybe my plane will be late, too, and I'll make it on time.

As another example, say you are afraid you cannot pay the rent on time this month. Talk yourself through your own "worst-case scenario." Ask yourself, "What is the worst thing that can happen if I don't pay the rent on time?" The landlord will be angry with me. Ask yourself, "Can I handle that?" Always answer YES. Then keep going. What will happen to my credit rating if he lets everyone know I didn't pay the rent on time? What if I can't pay the rent at all? What if he evicts me? After each answer acknowledge to yourself that you can handle it. When the landlord finally has you thrown in jail, your previous worries will not seem so dire. Perhaps you will realize unexpected solutions, such as a desire to find a better place to live and a nicer landlord. Whatever happens, you will feel better after this exercise and have a good laugh at yourself as well. And when in doubt, remember WWLD.

*Exercise 80*

## TRANSFORM IT TO A GIFT

### A Reminder to Live

Fears can limit you and stop you from living your life to its fullest. One of the most common fears is fear of death. Who wants to die without having fully lived? Think about the leaves in the fall. Why do they turn beautiful colors before letting go of the tree of life? God tells me He was just trying to raise money for the New England states, but I think there is more to it than that.

I think the colored leaves are telling us to stop being just another green leaf making the family tree happy by not being noticed or appearing unusual to the neighboring trees. When fall occurs they realize they have a limited time, they let go of the green and expose their uniqueness and beauty. They no longer care what anyone thinks.

Don't wait for fall to come before bursting into the unique colors of your life. Take this moment to accept your mortality and use this realization to free yourself to become your authentic self. One way to face your fear of death is to clarify what that really means, and you should do so now for this exercise. You can deal with specific fears and prepare for them. For instance, if you fear pain and suffering, isolation, extended medical treatments, or something else, you can talk to your health care providers, family, or spiritual advisor about exactly what decisions you'd like to make and what help you'll need. Put the appropriate resources in place now, and gather the courage to accept rather than deny your mortality. This will help you heal your life and live it fully in the time you have.

# EMOTIONAL 911

*Dealing with stress —
survivor behavior*

17

Each difficult moment has the potential to open
my eyes and open my heart.

— MYLA KABAT-ZINN

## Coaching Tip Seventeen

For me the number 911 represents two things. First, it is
the number to call in an emergency; second, it is the date
of the 2001 terrorist attacks that destroyed the Twin Tow-
ers in New York. When it comes to soul work, these asso-
ciations have some things in common. The biblical Jonah
didn't dial 911 when he was swallowed by the whale
because they don't make whale calls. But he also knew his
voice would be heard and his prayers answered. To quote
Jonah, "From the bowels of hell I cried out, and you
heard my voice." That is what true faith is about, and it
will get you through a 911 of any kind.

Disasters also help to remind us of our limited time here on this planet and how precious time is. During the 9/11 tragedy, think of all the cell phone calls made in those final moments to loved ones to say, "I love you." I hope you will accept your mortality and not let petty life experiences keep you from expressing your love. Anytime you leave home and return, say, "I love you."

A 911 crisis can also bring out the best in us as individuals and as a group. When one of us is hurt and in need, we all become a family. To maintain our emotional well-being, we must retain that sense of oneness, even when we are not being threatened by terrorists or emergencies.

Stress is a very real part of our daily life. We have to deal with stress by acting like survivors rather than victims. Survivors move, act, and express themselves rather than give up and give in. Survivors take action. I read recently about a brave elderly woman who was being robbed in her apartment and threatened to call 911. She then used the phone to strike the robber when he tried to get the phone away from her. The robber left her apartment very rapidly knowing he had encountered a survivor and not a victim.

Don't be afraid to ask for help when having your own emotional 911. Find the support people in your life who will be there for you in any situation. Also respond the way Jonah did and have faith in your spiritual resources.

The following exercises will help you to have healthy resources to deal with stressful and emotionally challenging events in your life.

## *Exercise 81*

## CHOCOLATE BUZZ

Stimulate Your Endorphins

If you are feeling low, a great way to lift your mood is to eat chocolate. I always recommend eating chocolate ice cream for a pick-me-up. It makes you feel loved and happy. Chocolate is a great cure for the everyday blues. So for this exercise, just keep a bag of dark chocolates around or a tub of chocolate ice cream, and anytime you are feeling as though you need some TLC, have some chocolate! Believe it or not, if not overdone, chocolate is good for you physically and emotionally.

What most people don't realize is that chocolate ice cream comes in many shapes and sizes in our lives. Ask yourself what your life's chocolate ice cream is, and the answer will help you discover where your life should be going and what you should be doing with your time.

## Exercise *82*

### BE YOUR OWN HOTLINE

How to Find the Answer

The next time you are feeling emotional distress, try this: imagine that there is an emotional hotline that has all of the answers for you. Call it, and imagine what the person on the other end of the line would say. What questions and steps would the person suggest to help you through your problem, whether you're feeling grief, sadness, loneliness, guilt, or something else? In fact, this type of emotional hotline is available to you whenever you take the time to listen.

If my mother answers the phone, you probably would not be very happy with her answer. As a teenager it drove me nuts to come home and tell my mom what terrible things happened to me that day at school. Her answer was always the same, "God is redirecting you. Something good will come of this." I figured it was her away to avoid having to deal with my troubles. So off I went to my room to talk to God instead, shutting the door so no one could hear me and think I was psychotic. Talking to God is another way to characterize this emotional support hotline.

It took me a while to realize what a gift my mom's advice was. She changed my view of the future and gave me hope. Many times when something I wanted to happen didn't, I was led to a better situation than I could have hoped for. So keep your hotline open and watch what happens.

# *Exercise 83*

## RITUAL

### Emotional Cleansing

When you deny your feelings and emotions, your body will be affected and begin to break down. But if you stop being the good child to please others, and express appropriate anger, you will start on a path toward understanding, forgiveness, health, and wellness.

You can also heal your past by voicing unexpressed emotions. For this exercise, think of a difficult event or relationship in your life; perhaps it is something you feel guilty for having done or it is a person you have been unable to forgive. Now take a piece of paper and write down any negative feelings, whether toward yourself or toward the other person. Then visualize a ritual in which you sail out on a lake and throw your negative thoughts overboard. Or, build a fire and toss the sheets of paper containing your negative feelings into the flames and watch them burn up. After you have let go, notice how different you feel. Now visualize the person you are having a problem with and surround the person with love, forgiveness, and acceptance. Remember to forgive yourself, too.

Repeat this ritual as many times as it takes until you really feel the shift within you. The next time you meet the person involved, you will experience a change in your relationship. Consciousness is not local, and you have made a difference with your efforts.

## *Exercise 84*

### LISTEN TO MUSIC

#### Let It Carry You

We all make music during our daily life. Stop and listen, and you will realize sound surrounds us all the time. Rather than adding distraction to your life by watching TV or listening to the news, use music to bring focus and deepen your emotions. Music also helps you to learn, and I play it in the operating room to help both patients and staff. Plus, I know for a fact that not watching the news will make you healthier and allow you to sleep better.

For this exercise, try listening to different types of music. Find what type of music creates a feeling of peace and well-being for you. When you are in stressful situations, play this music, such as in the car while driving. When you want to relax, turn on this music instead of the TV. Listen to the music of your soul and heal — that's why they call it soul music; it carries a message. Find harmony through the music you love, and let it carry you through the day.

# *Exercise 85*

## DRINKS ARE ON ME

### The Elixir of Life

Take a friend out for a drink. And when you do, drink in each other's words and presence. Support for the soul is not always crafted in a crisis, but in the little moments that build relationships. For this exercise, you can go out for a cup of coffee or tea or for a beer or glass of red wine; you can go to a coffee shop, a bar, or a park to share a warm thermos. The point, however, is not to load up on caffeine or alcohol for an artificial high, but to share the elixir of life and what it provides.

Experience the time and words you share with a friend or family member. Every morning, I stop by one of our children's houses to share a cup of coffee, but more importantly we share our love, worries, feelings, insights, and touch. This time together allows us to share our lives and helps us to survive. We drink in each other's words and digest them without prejudice or judgment. By listening we help each other to heal.

For this exercise, the first one's on me — provided it's not from a rare bottle of wine you got at an auction. Take in those you care about by taking them out, and shower them with love the way players drench one another in champagne after winning a championship together.

# FLEX YOUR
# CREATIVE MUSCLES

*Create a work of art with the
material at hand*

Creativity requires the courage to let go of certainties.

— **ERICH FROMM**

## Coaching Tip Eighteen

Creative expression plays a very important role in keeping your life balanced and healthy. My creativity has been expressed primarily through writing and painting. Both have played prominent roles in my life. The manner in which you express your creativity may vary, but it is important that you pursue a creative outlet.

Do not be afraid to attempt new forms of expression. You might think that you can't draw a straight line or write an interesting sentence, but let me give you some hope. The worst grade I received in four years of college was a C in Creative Writing. Even though I have written bestsellers, I can't get Colgate University to raise my grade so I can graduate with high honors. Why did I get a poor grade? Because I was a science major who wrote from his head and not his heart. I still need editing when I get into that place and start writing sermons.

You must truly see in order to write or paint a face, a tree, or anything else. In my opinion, artists and writers are able to see the world and their surroundings in greater detail. They are able to describe and portray life through their art. I have been painting since I was a child, and I actually went into surgery so my skillful hands would not be wasted. An operation can be a work of art, too. I can recall how in awe I was of the beauty of the human body — we are very colorful on the inside.

When you tap into your creative lens, you learn to see and become aware of how beautiful all of God's creations are. Look into a flower and see the minute things within it that make it what it is. There is a true artist behind creation, believe me.

How and why does expressing your creativity help you to heal? For two reasons: First, when you do something that makes you lose track of time, you enter a trance state and are ageless and free of all physical awareness and afflictions. Second, when you express feelings, be they in words or images, what is trapped within you is brought to the surface so you are able to heal both emotionally and physically.

Be sure to leave time in your life to create works of

art. They can be anything from a small doodle to a fine art painting, from a short poem to a beautiful garden, a meaningful relationship, or a great novel — it doesn't matter. The following exercises will help you to unleash your creative flow and discover new ways to express yourself.

## *Exercise 86*

## MAKE A COLLAGE

### Celebrate Your Life with Pictures

Collages are an interesting and simple way to create art and explore your life. By cutting and pasting symbols, pictures, and objects together you are capable of creating something new out of your experience.

Our kitchen is like a collage because the cabinets are covered with photos, family notes, newspaper clippings, awards, graduation programs, and birth, death, and wedding announcements. I always feel that by keeping the house the way it has been since our children were young, we remain young. Why grow old when you can grow young?

For this exercise, either make a personal collage about your life or make an ongoing, public collage, like the one in our kitchen, that celebrates your family and friends. For the personal collage, buy some poster board and cover it with pictures, magazine or newspaper articles, words of wisdom, and anything else that inspires, motivates, empowers, or touches you. You can have an overall theme for the collage or just cut and paste anything that's important to you. Display what you make in your kitchen, bedroom, or office. To display a family collage, get a bulletin board or use magnets to cover metal cabinets or a refrigerator with all the happenings in your and your family's life. You are creating a shrine dedicated to those you love, so make it interesting!

# *Exercise 87*

## FREEWRITE

### Create a Short Story

Every life is a story, but most of them never get told or written about. Now is the time for you to write a story, either a real or fictional one. Actually, I really don't consider anything fiction because all stories come from the experience, both conscious and unconscious, of the author. What writing does is give the writer a gift. By expressing yourself, you release the emotions that need to be expressed, which allows you to live a healthier life. Many studies reveal the benefit of journaling, story-telling, and writing.

I will never forget meeting Mario Puzo, the author of *The Godfather*, and talking to him about writing. He said he would sit and wait for the character he was writing about to speak to him and tell him what to write. In other words, he became the people he wrote about.

For this exercise, write a story. Write it for yourself, your family, or the world. Write for any age group. What do you need to say? Grab a pad and pencil or sit down at the computer and get going. Don't worry about spelling or grammar — just let it all out. Turn off the thinking mode in your head and let the ideas flow through you. If it's easier to write about a fictional character, do so, or it might feel more natural to describe a colorful person in your life. Choose an event or an emotional experience, humorous or sad, and document it for posterity.

Share your stories with family and see if you can get them started with storytelling and writing. Some of the most important stories always come from senior citizens. They have a lifetime stored within.

# Exercise 88

## PHOTOGRAPHY

### Real Life as Art

I learned from a patient who was a landscape gardener how beautiful nature and life can be. John had cancer, and when I couldn't cure his cancer with surgery, he refused further treatment and went home from the hospital. He said, "You forgot something. It's springtime, and I am going home to make the world beautiful before I die." To make a long story short, he died, but it was decades later at the age of ninety-four, and with no sign of cancer. John taught me how beautiful the world is. He would point out to me the tiniest blossoms I never would have noticed, and it changed the way I saw the world. I started bringing flowering weeds home to plant in our yard. Beauty can be found everywhere.

Most of us are not talented artists or authors who can re-create this beauty, so get a camera and go for a walk in nature. See the beauty and take some awe-inspiring pictures. Look down at the flowers, but also up at the sky, at the trees, at the ocean, and at the people and living things around you. They are like flowers, too. Each of us is unique and beautiful in our own way, just as you are. You will find the more you look and photograph, the more you see, and the more beautiful the world becomes.

So carry your camera with you and record the wonders of creation. Take the beauty with you wherever you go, and store it within your heart.

## *Exercise 89*

## PAINT A MURAL

### Enhance Your Environment

In one of the recovery rooms in the hospital where I worked I once painted a mural. The mural contained a penguin with a stethoscope listening to a hatching egg, a fish tank, birds, rainbows, and much more. This particular room is where children are kept as they awaken from anesthesia, and I felt it would ease the children's pain, fear, and confusion if, when they awakened, they saw this painting. I also once volunteered to do a mural at the drive-up window of our bank, so people would be less aggravated as they waited in their car wondering why things were moving so slowly.

Think of all the places you spend time working, waiting, and living. How could you make your world a more creative and healing place? For this exercise, choose one space to paint a mural. With inspiration, you can change your life and the lives of those around you. You may want to start in your home — perhaps in a child's bedroom or playroom. Then consider places in your work environment and in the community where a mural would be welcome. Paint some works of art for people to see to reduce their stress and tension when they step out into the world; put a mural wherever you want positive energy to flow. If creating a mural on your own is daunting, consider joining a community service program where you can paint murals to beautify a neighborhood near you.

## *Exercise 90*

## BE CREATIVE WITH THE SCRAPS

### Hands On!

I never throw anything out because the artist in me won't allow it. I save car parts, tools, toys, pieces of wood, windows, and everything else you can think of. What do I do with them? I build things for our children and grandchildren, our pets, and my wife and I to enjoy and play with. Is our yard and home rather strange looking? Yes. But do the kids and animals appreciate it? Yes, they really do.

The kids love the tree house I made out of old lumber and windows, and the pets love to climb over the platforms I made for them in and out of the house. Our house is also full of things our children made when they were growing up, and our living room and their bedrooms are filled with everything from models to sculptures.

For this exercise, become a found-object sculptor yourself. Gather interesting things from around the house or look for them at garage sales. Do not be afraid to become a creator and build something for someone in your life out of the scraps available at hand. Build something for the house and something for outdoors — anything that will enhance the world. For instance, the birds will appreciate a nice new home or feeder, and all kids enjoy a little house or slide.

CHAPTER

# BALANCING ACT

*You have needs, too*

The best and safest thing is to keep a balance in your life, acknowledge the great powers around us and in us. If you can do that, and live that way, you are really a wise man.

— EURIPIDES

## Coaching Tip Nineteen

How do you keep a balance in your life between your individual needs and the world around you? Brian Dyson, CEO of Coca-Cola Enterprises, shares his idea: "Imagine life as a game in which you are juggling five balls into the air: work, family, health, friends, and spirit....Work is a rubber ball; if you drop it, it will bounce back....Family, health, friends, and spirit are made of glass. If you drop one of these, they will be irrevocably scuffed, marked, nicked, damaged, or even shattered....You must understand that and strive for balance in your life."

When your life is out of balance, no one's needs get met, including your own. In order to find balance you need to discover what your own needs and limits are first. Once you do that, you can make decisions, say no when you need to, and schedule your time without guilt, shame, or blame. Years ago, our five children didn't like my occupation. I was on call as a surgeon and not always available to participate in their lives. I can remember running a Cub Scout meeting from the operating room by yelling into a telephone the nurse was holding for me. (Be assured that the patient was well taken care of.) One night I came home and announced, "I'm home and ready to be with my children." They told me they were busy and had plans to go roller-skating at a nearby rink. I pointed out that if they could go roller-skating, then I had the right to be a surgeon. We didn't have to feel guilty about what was right for each of us. I learned that I couldn't be a dad, surgeon, husband, scout leader, son, and pet owner simultaneously; I had to be me.

There are times when work feels right because it is your way of finding meaning and contributing to the world, and there are times when it is just plain wrong. The truth is that there will be times in your life when you need to listen to your own needs and make your own path, times when it is right to follow the paths of others, and times when, by choice, you will share a path and common destination. The following exercises will help you learn to keep your needs a priority and maintain a balance between what others need and what is best for you.

# *Exercise 91*
## BALANCE YOUR GOALS
Develop a Well-Rounded Life

In today's modern world, if you were to build a house, it is likely that you would choose more than one substance with which to construct it. Wouldn't you incorporate a variety of materials to make the house the finest and safest structure you could? Of course you would — because by using a balance of materials you provide your home with a necessary combination of strength, durability, and comfort.

So too with your personal goals. For this exercise, you will make a plan for building your life that contains a strong foundation and a structure that can withstand the elements of time and nature. Make a list of what goals you seek to achieve spiritually, physically, and materially. Is there a balance between these facets of your life? Try to place equal importance on all parts of yourself and your world. Notice where you are out of balance, or where you are lacking goals or focus. Make another list of the goals that will help you to have a more well-rounded life. Focus on the areas that have the highest priority first.

When you do this, you are helping to create your life by defining your priorities. If you rely too heavily upon one aspect of life, you won't be properly supported, and you may fall before your time.

## *Exercise 92*
# UNCLUTTER YOUR LIFE

### Create Harmony

Ultimately, we can't control anything but our thoughts. So instead of trying to control events, we should work to establish order by creating harmony. Harmony comes when we find a sense of rhythm in our lives, whatever the pace or intensity of the music. Some like to go a hundred miles an hour and others twenty-five. Go at a comfortable pace for you.

One way to find harmony is to listen to your needs and desires in each moment, rather than living in anticipation of the next. For this exercise, get rid of your lists for at least a week. I used to have lists and schedules so I could fit things into my uncontrolled life as an on-call surgeon. In time, I realized the schedules and lists only created more problems for me, so I threw them all out. I began to live in the moment, doing what felt right and what needed to be done.

Look around your home and office and dispose of all the unnecessary notes telling you what to do and when to do it. Don't throw out critical information about important work meetings and events, but get rid of the craziness of little notes and reminders on the fridge, counter, mirror, desk, and so on. Clean them up! Especially throw out any list that has been sitting around for a month. Clutter in your mind is as distracting as clutter in your environment, and it blocks the natural feeling of harmony.

## *Exercise 93*
## MAKING CHANGES

### What If?

If you knew you had one year to live, what changes would you make in your life? I've seen how a life-threatening illness often inspires people to transform their lives for the better, so for this exercise, pretend you are facing one. In truth, none of us really knows how much time we have, but if you knew you had only one more year, what would you do?

I want you to think of all of the changes you'd make, large and small, and write them down. Would you stop worrying about how you looked and what other people thought? Would you buy a new house? Find a meaningful job? Learn to say no to others and yes to yourself? Would you express feelings you have been holding inside or ask for help?

What changes would you make in your lifestyle so that your physical, spiritual, and emotional needs were met? Include some very basic, practical things, such as making out a will and giving away treasures. Then include the joyful events that you have put off for too long.

How about getting a dog? Moving to the mountains or seashore? Laughing more? Caring for yourself and your diet and health? Spending time with those you love? Taking your tie off and abandoning the dress code?

When you identify the things that make life precious for you, make a decision to include them in your life now. Make your short-term plans as satisfying as your long-term plans.

# *Exercise 94*
## FIND THE RIGHT PATH

Way to Go?

I once went for a walk after a snowstorm and discovered that it was hard to create my own path through the thick snow. The following day it was easier to make my way because I had my footprints to walk in. But the day after that everything was frozen and icy, and my footprints were risky to step in because if I did not fit into them perfectly, I could fall and break my leg. I was forced to create a new path. In other words, what might be the right path one day may be completely wrong the next. Maintaining balance in your life is not just about avoiding falling down. It requires knowing which path to take and being prepared for every condition.

Are you walking a balanced path in your life? Is there an equal amount of confidence and wariness, giving and taking? Close your eyes and see your life as a path you are walking. Look forward and back. Are you creating your own way or only following others? Both can be right at different times, but you should be the one who decides when to go your way and when to follow in the footsteps of others.

Then, consider your footwear. Take all your shoes out of the closet. Do you have what you need to help you on your trail through life? Now consider, who in your life embodies your shoes? Who helps you make it through the snow, mud, and other obstacles life presents?

Make a list of this equipment and these people. These are the resources that will assist you to make the right footprint in life and keep your balance when out trail-blazing — so you can eventually become a guide for others.

# *Exercise 95*
## PLAY FRISBEE
### Breaking Out of Your Routine

A well-balanced person is more likely to withstand the forces of nature than one who is unbalanced or relying on one resource to help him or her stand and survive the elements. Often we focus on one thing that we want to achieve and forget to develop as a human being. Professional athletes and their coaches understand that to succeed they need to develop not one set of muscles but all of them. They know they need to be comprehensive and find balance because the body is a unit; each part relies on the strengths and abilities of the others.

For a month, work a new set of muscles. Develop your abilities and make a point of doing things you normally would not do. Play Frisbee, go bowling, or play outside with your dog. Find activities that give you pure enjoyment and the sensation of truly living. Even the smallest changes can begin to develop your capacities. Brush your teeth with the opposite hand. Shave or comb your hair in a different way. Enter and leave your house through a different door. How many unthinking, tiny ruts have you gotten into? Altering these just a little can improve your skills and balance. Finally, practice walking on a narrow beam of wood. Develop and strengthen your physical ability to balance. With practice you can become who you want to be as an athlete, spouse, parent, and friend.

CHAPTER **THE OBSTACLE COURSE OF LIFE**

*There are no mistakes*

For a long time it had seemed to me that life was about to begin — real life. But there was always some obstacle in the way, something to be gotten through first, some unfinished business, time still to be served, or a debt to be paid. Then life would begin. At last it dawned on me that these obstacles were my life.

— ALFRED D. SOUZA

## Coaching Tip Twenty

No matter what the circumstances of your life, you always have a choice about how you perceive them. Life can be seen as an obstacle course filled with hurdles or a marathon you are determined to complete. The same experience, be it a race or a disease, will be experienced differently by each individual. You decide how the experience will affect you based upon your attitude toward life.

I see life as a circle. Having been through a past-life experience, I am touched by the literalness of this analogy. We live, die, and return to this world, though the reasons for this are mysterious. Are we here to complete the circle of life and reconnect with each other to work out our lives and become who and what we were meant to be? If so, why do we have to keep recycling ourselves? Why can't we do it on the first go-around? I think it has to do with life being a school. If you are in the lower grades, it's going to take some time for you to achieve enlightenment and graduate.

Everyone needs to answer for themselves what they are here to do. What are you looking for? What will allow you to feel at peace when you achieve your destination? What are you here to accomplish and do in your lifetime to give it meaning? It isn't about accumulating a certain amount of things, because when you do, you will just find something else you want. What is the destination that can bring us the peace we seek?

The circle of love is the true goal, and we need true teachers and guides to show us the way. In this material world, we can sometimes migrate from place to place and job to job looking for it, until we realize that the sky above us is the same everywhere we go and that the earth beneath our feet may change but it doesn't change us. The journey and the destination both exist inside of us, and all the exercises in this book are meant to help you see and walk that path of the soul.

In addition, while external teachers are important — those people who teach us to embody love rather than seek it — the most important teacher is also inside yourself. I know I have gotten directions from a voice that I hear when I take the time to be by myself. Perhaps all we need to do is be silent and hear that still, small voice and follow the directions we receive — instead of arguing with it because we think we know the right way to go. When you change your attitude and orientation, when you stop resisting, the obstacle course becomes your teacher and the mountainous hurdles shrink. You achieve the peak and find it is all downhill from there. Amen. May it be so for you all.

## *Exercise 96*

### FORM A CIRCLE

Talking Stick

There are many people and fellow travelers on this journey of life who are looking for support, direction, and love. Find some like-minded people and put together a circle gathering. Choose a place to meet out in nature or in a quiet environment. It is best not to be in someone's home, so you can avoid the distractions and disruptions of everyday life. One of the benefits of this exercise is that you separate yourself from the demands of cell phones and the needs of others.

Then choose and bring a sacred object, like a carved stick or feather. Assemble the group into a circle. Begin with a period of silence, and then do some chanting or a meditation together. While you do this, ask each person to listen to his or her inner voice: What things have they never said but need to say, and what questions have they wanted answered but never asked?

When everyone is ready, hand the sacred object to the shortest person in the circle and let that person begin, sharing whatever he or she wants with the circle. The role of the circle is to listen to the speaker; no one should comment on, doubt, question, or answer what is said. By listening to the speaker without commenting, the circle provides the opportunity for the person speaking to find the answers within him- or herself. Then continue passing the sacred object around the circle until each person has had a chance to share his or her thoughts and feelings safely within the circle.

# *Exercise 97*
## HONOR YOUR RELATIONSHIPS

### Rings of Life

Do you know the origin of wedding rings? Some say they go back 4,800 years to the ancient Egyptians, who are generally credited with the genesis of wedding band exchanges. The Egyptians twisted reedy plants, like hemp, into rings that they believed were linked to supernatural, immortal love, forming a circle with no end. Like a mandala, the circle is symbolic of our wholeness. The Romans upgraded to iron, but for Roman women, wedding bands signified a binding legal agreement of ownership by their husbands, who regarded rings as tokens of purchase. Nice guys. Both the Egyptians and Romans wore bands on the fourth finger of the left hand because they swore the vena amoris, or love vein, connected directly from that finger to the heart, thereby joining a couple's destiny. Modern wedding rings continue to symbolize the perfect unity of love, with no beginning and no end. For some, they are symbolic of holiness, perfection, and peace, as well as the sun, earth, and universe.

How many people do you know who are part of your life and in essence wedded to you and your well-being? I have only one wife, but I wear three wedding rings. One relates to our marriage of over fifty years. The second was made by a friend and has a rose on it, my mother's name. It relates to my marriage and to my friends and family. The third was made by one of our sons, and it relates to my special relationship with our children. I wear the latter on the fourth finger of my right hand, so all the rings fit.

Now imagine a giant ring surrounding you and all the people you love. Notice who is in the circle with you and who you have left out. When was the last time you said thank you to these people for being there for and with you? What can you do now to honor the relationships you have with these people? When you are done, draw a family circle and connect everyone. Then call or email everyone and share your feelings. Connect with your circle of life.

# *Exercise 98*

## MAKE A SURVIVAL KIT

### What to Pack

Nearly every day we face situations that can make us uncomfortable. From appearing in court, getting on a plane, and going to the dentist to visiting a sick friend in the hospital, there are many times when a survival kit would be helpful. When you face an uncomfortable situation, bring along some support. Numerous studies reveal how much less pain is experienced by those who have support, whether you are delivering a baby or receiving an injection.

For this exercise, think of the situations that typically make you sweat, and make up a survival kit for each one. For each circumstance, choose an appropriate carrying case — such as a briefcase, backpack, lunch box, or gift bag — and place in it the items you think you'll need. When you visit a sick or troubled friend, bring your love, laughter, and ability to listen, and maybe some chocolate chip cookies. If big parties make you nervous, bring along some affirmations or jokes in your bag.

If you get anxious getting on a plane, remember first that you have choices. You can decide not to go or to travel some other way. But also, bring your survival kit along and stuff it with guided imagery of a successful, uneventful flight, as well as music, food, and books to read. Try to fly with a friend or family member who will be there when you have a panic attack.

We all need survival kits to help us through the obstacles of life. So make up a few for the next time you need a bit of support.

# *Exercise 99*
## LOVE YOURSELF
### Honor the Whole Reflection

I have found meaning in my life in a very heartfelt way — by learning to love myself and others and to take that love out into the world and share it. Loving and being loved helps get you and the person you love through the tough times. Loving thyself as you love thy neighbor can be a challenge. You may find it hard to love yourself. If you do, examine what thoughts and feelings stand in the way of loving yourself, because if you cannot do that, you cannot love others.

For this exercise, stand in front of a mirror. You can learn to love the person you see even if you don't like everything about yourself. Perfection is not necessary for love. Start with one part of yourself that you love and say into the mirror: I love my hair, my skin, eyes, and so on. Do this every day for a month, and each day add another part of you that you love. Move on to the qualities you possess. Keep looking in the mirror until you love the whole reflection. If you truly loved yourself, what changes would you make in your life now?

## *Exercise 100*

### REST TIME

Doing Nothing Is Doing Something

Do you feel guilty when you take time to rest? Even God took a day off when He was creating everything, so why can't you? Know that doing no thing is still doing some thing. When you stop doing and take time just to be, it can be inspiring, healing, and renewing.

All travelers need to rest on their journey. When was the last time you stopped to rest and restore yourself? To rest does not mean you are doing nothing. Resting is an activity. For one week, practice listening to your body, and when it is tired, rest. Make sure you get enough rest during the night as well. The body needs its time to work and its time to heal, so balance your exercise and work time with plenty of rest and sleep. During each of these activities your physiology varies. The same hormones that stimulate our immune system make us sleepy. So listen to your body and follow its rhythm.

Take your naps, and when in doubt about what to do — lie down and think about it! And if you doze off, you'll dream up an answer to what needs to be done.

## *Exercise 101*

### SEEK INNER PEACE

Final Exam

What are you looking for? If you are unable to define what you are looking for, how will you know when you find it? There are times on the journey when you may feel a deep sense of anxiety. Carl Jung used the term "gnawing unrest" to describe this. When I am in this state, I do not get upset. Instead, as you know, I think of it as I do hunger — as something that will lead me to seek nourishment. I know I need to find the reason for the unrest to resolve the feeling and once again achieve the peace of mind I constantly seek.

We often forget that the wisdom we seek is already within us. Even though it can be scary, the most illuminating place we can go is within ourselves. It takes courage to look at ourselves and to listen to the voice inside us, yet only by turning within can we find inner peace.

I came across this quiz in a newsletter. It is one of my favorites. Take the time to monitor your progress through life by reviewing these questions. Use them to guide you toward reclaiming your peace of mind. This is your last and most important exercise.

*Some signs and symptoms of inner peace:*
- A tendency to think and act spontaneously rather than on fears based on past experiences

- An unmistakable ability to enjoy each moment
- A loss of interest in judging other people
- A loss of interest in judging self
- A loss of interest in interpreting the actions of others
- A loss of interest in conflict
- A loss of ability to worry (this is a very serious symptom)
- Frequent, overwhelming episodes of appreciation
- Contented feelings of connectedness with others and nature
- Frequent attacks of smiling
- An increasing tendency to let things happen rather than make them happen
- An increased susceptibility to the love extended by others as well as the uncontrollable urge to extend it

WARNING: If you have some or all of the above symptoms, please be advised that your condition of inner peace may be so far advanced as to not be curable and may lead to love blindness. If you are exposed to anyone exhibiting any of these symptoms, remain exposed at your own risk.

# ABOUT THE AUTHOR

Dr. Bernie S. Siegel is a well-known proponent of alternative approaches to healing that heal not just the body, but the mind and soul as well. Bernie, as his friends and patients call him, studied medicine at Colgate University and Cornell University Medical College. His surgical training took place at Yale New Haven Hospital, West Haven Veteran's Hospital, and the Children's Hospital of Pittsburgh. In 1978 Bernie pioneered a new approach to group and individual cancer therapy called ECaP (Exceptional Cancer Patients) that utilized patients' drawings, dreams, and feelings, and broke new ground in facilitating important patient lifestyle changes and engaging the patient in the healing process. Bernie retired from general and pediatric surgical practice in 1989.

Always a strong advocate for his patients, Bernie has since dedicated himself to humanizing the medical establishment's approach to patients and empowering patients to play a great role in the healing process. He is an active speaker, traveling around the world to address patient and caregiver groups. As the author of several books, including *Love, Medicine & Miracles, Peace, Love & Healing, How to Live Between Office Visits,* and *Prescriptions for Living,* Bernie has been at the forefront of the medical ethics and spiritual issues of our day. He and his wife (and occasional coauthor), Bobbie, live in a suburb of New Haven, Connecticut. They have five children and eight grandchildren.